Managing potentials in food and beverage control

A food and beverage control system

Managing potentials in food and beverage control

A food and beverage control system

Horst B Gümmer

Edward Arnold

First published in Great Britain 1983
by Edward Arnold (Publishers) Ltd
41 Bedford Square
London WC1 3DQ

Edward Arnold (Australia) Pty Ltd
80 Waverley Road
Caulfield East
Victoria 3145

British Library Cataloguing in Publication Data

Gümmer, Horst B
Managing potentials in food and beverage control.
1. Food and service management
I. Title
647'.95'068 TX911.3.M27

ISBN 0-7131-0732-4

Text set in 10/11 Times Roman by The Castlefield Press, Moulton, Northants
Printed and bound in Great Britain by Biddles Ltd, Guildford and King's Lynn

Contents

Foreword

The responsibilities of a Food and Beverage Manager (or Catering Manager) are many and they vary very much from one establishment to another in the hotel and catering industry, depending on the size of the organisation and other factors. However, with the constant changes, new legislation, and developments in the catering industry, the Catering Manager carries an ever-increasing burden of responsibilities that demand the widest possible knowledge and the best leadership. He must have the technical knowledge of catering, he must know of the principles of production and service of food and beverages, and of the underlying processes, commodities, requirements, sources of their supply and of the methods of catering operations. He must also be aware of any computer technology. Finally, he should have managerial knowledge and know of administrative skills and techniques, accounting, costing, marketing and the principles of general personnel management. This knowledge makes him competent to plan, organise and control. These are the three main functions of management.

In any industry you must plan ahead and have the organisation ready, set standards and install the controls before you start operating. Once business is started the manager must continue to watch and improve in order to establish whether the control system suits the operation and produces useful information. Only with such information will he be able to make sound decisions and improve business performance faster than ever before.

Food and beverage control in the hotel and catering industry is no exception.

Horst B Gümmer

1 The calculation of food and beverage costs

The calculation of the cost of food and beverages as a percentage of sales is used by the majority of managers in the hotel and catering industry as a way of assessing performance. They will usually use the figures to compare current performance with that of a past period or with general standards in the industry. It is the most commonly used method of monitoring food and beverage cost.

The caterer is usually satisfied if the cost percentage does not fluctuate greatly, if it is close to his original budget estimate and if it falls within a range of typical food and beverage cost percentages for similar operations. For example, typical food and cost percentages for a variety of kinds of operation are:

Restaurants	30–35%
Coffee shops	35–40%
Cafeterias	40–45%
Fast food restaurants	35–40%
Country clubs	40–50%

It is, however, much more enlightening and important to achieve a comparison of the *actual* food cost with the *potential* food costs. How many managers, I wonder, know what their potential food cost and potential profit is? Have you ever asked yourself why a bar or restaurant has a worse cost percentage than it should? If this does happen, are you able to identify which part of the operation and which food or drink items are causing it to happen?

Control of food and beverage costs is greatly helped by speed and accuracy. Do you have to wait for two days for a weekly stocktake result, or do you even have a monthly stocktake? You should have a system which allows, in a short time, a cost and price percentage analysis for each item, group of items, and sales outlet. You can save money by acting quickly on the basis of up-to-date and accurate information.

In this book I will demonstrate the stages of calculation and the uses of actual and potential food and beverage costs.

2 The principles of food and beverage control

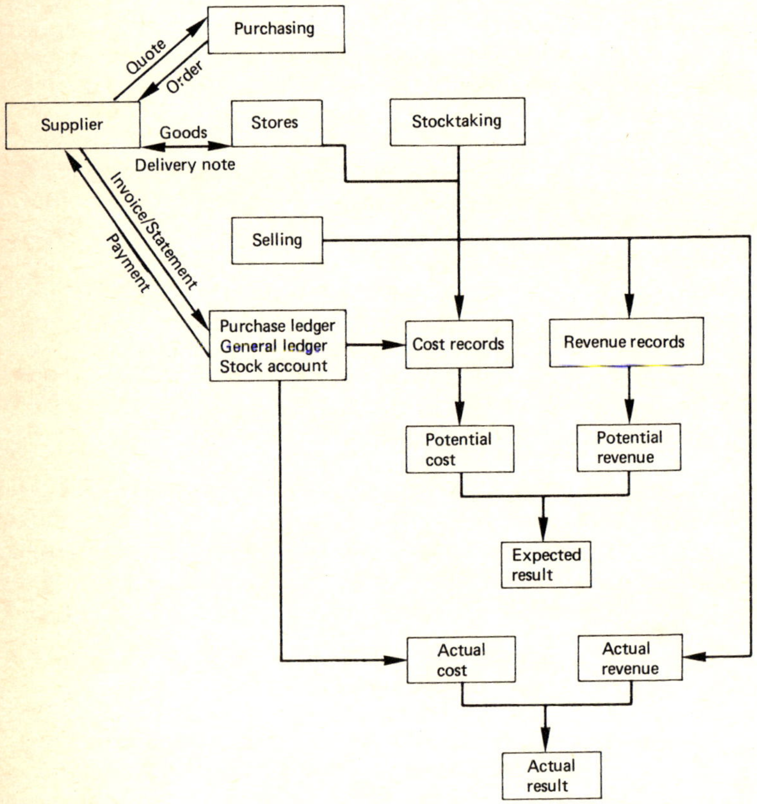

1 The principles of food and beverage control

The diagram above shows the main processes and principles involved in a control system. It is very important that the manager *and* his staff know the outline of this system. If staff know how the actual and potential results are produced they can be of much greater help in ensuring a good result.

A brief summary of the system

1 When goods must be purchased, the purchaser contacts suppliers, receives quotations and subsequently confirms an order to a chosen supplier.
2 The supplier sends goods accompanied by a delivery note. They are taken by the purchaser into his stores where they, and their costs, are recorded.
3 The goods are later requisitioned from the stores, as needed, by all units, unless they were originally delivered to and stored in a separate unit.
4 The costs of all goods must be carefully recorded. They are essential to stocktaking procedures in order to work out the potential cost.
5 The first cost record, the goods inward record, along with all delivery notes go to the purchase ledger and then to the general ledger where they form the stock account.
6 Invoices are sent by the supplier to the purchase ledger where they are married up with delivery notes and order forms. When they have been checked together a cheque for payment is sent to the supplier. The payment made to the supplier is the actual cost. This may differ slightly from the cost first recorded from goods inward because discounts or credits can reduce the cost. Pilferage or wastage can result in a higher cost.
7 The selling is done through sales outlets or units which have requisitioned the products from the stores. The revenue from sales is recorded in cash registers or on bills. This information forms the basis of a sales analysis from which the potential revenue is calculated.
8 The record of potential revenue and potential cost allows us to calculate the potential or expected result.
9 Actual revenue is what is received in cash or credit form. We use this and actual cost to calculate our actual results.
10 Potential and actual results are both derived from the same stock figures.

Ideally, the potential revenue and actual revenue should be identical but this is not so in reality. There are many possible reasons why discrepancies occur and these will be discussed later in the book. Potential and actual results are both derived from the same stock, revenue and purchase figures after allowing for certain items, such as discounts, credits, breakages and staff meals. One can assume, therefore, that any differentials which occur show a lack of control and that thorough investigation is needed to find and rectify any loopholes. An understanding of these principles will also be of great help in making a decision about computerisation and in choosing the kind of system that is best suited to the needs of an operation.

3 Purchasing

You should remember that good buying is the first step to profit and so purchasing decisions and procedures must be very carefully thought about and controlled. Because of the importance of purchasing, only the Food and Beverage Manager, a qualified Purchasing Officer, or a Chef should be in charge. The purchaser ought to be conversant with all the products and their sources and be able to negotiate and have the legal knowledge any sensible buyer should have. The two main requisites for successful purchasing are purchasing specifications and standard purchasing procedures.

Purchase specifications

This should include the weight, quality and origin of the product and the weight, content and size of the packaging. For example, purchase specification for tomatoes might be:

> Good red colour, well formed, 2 ounces each.
> Free from decay.
> Weight 12lbs net, 14lbs gross.
> Count – approximately 96 tomatoes.
> English preferred.

This purchase specification ensures that all know what is expected, enables accurate price comparisons and ensures that the quality of product does not vary.

Standard purchasing procedures

When choosing a supplier the following factors must be considered:

1 Prices.
2 Discounts – *but* be careful of overbuying prompted by bulk discount.
3 Minimum order levels.
4 Delivery procedures.
5 Order procedures – does the supplier phone you or do you phone him?
6 The quality of product.
7 The supplier's reputation.

8 Part order deliveries or standing orders. Special attention should be given to part order deliveries if they cannot be avoided (see page 6).

Furthermore, the following points must also be considered before orders are placed.

1 Classification of products.
2 Purchase orders must be confirmed in writing.
3 Who is responsible for purchasing?
4 Stock life of products.
5 Cash flow. The money available to market purchasers.

The quantity needed depends on a number of factors:

1 Existing stock levels.
2 The expected volume of business.
3 Current market prices and trends.
4 Tariffs.
5 Storage space available.

Having taken all these factors into account, the purchaser must anticipate what products can be sold. A sales mix analysis will enable him to see what is selling and to discard what is not selling. Stocktaking will allow him to know what gross profit each item is generating. These considerations allow him to set re-order levels and order size bearing in mind sales volume and delivery frequency. You must remember that:

1 Holding stock costs money.
2 Orders must be controlled.
3 The higher the stock level the greater is the danger of spoilage and stock loss, and the longer and more difficult are stocktaking procedures.

The responsibility for buying wet or dry goods items should, in my opinion, be the responsibility of the Head Chef. The purchasing of food is a very specialised task which requires an expert knowledge and a systematic approach if the changing day-to-day requirements of differing departments are to be handled successfully. The Head Chef and his staff will be able to ensure that the correct quality is supplied and that the standard of product remains constant. If, however, the Food and Beverage Manager or Purchasing Officer is to be responsible, all decisions should be made in close liaison with the Head Chef.

To summarise:

1 All purchases must be made through a nominated person – Manager, Officer, or Chef.
2 A standard purchase order form should be utilised for wet stock, dry stock and cellar goods (see pages 7 and 8).
3 The Manager or Head Chef should be the only person to authorise purchase orders *before* the order is placed.
4 It is an important principle of control that the same person should not order *and* receive the goods.

5 Up-to-date prices from a variety of supplies should be regularly obtained and compared.
6 Watch the market for special offers.
7 If possible, see and taste goods before ordering.
8 Compare the prices you pay with the food cost indices provided in the trade press.
9 Give precise specifications when ordering including the unit price and total value of the order.
10 When orders are placed by phone, a purchase order must also be completed.
11 Cash purchases should always be discouraged. If necessary a procedure should be established to set authorisation limits.
12 All items ordered according to purchase specification must be recorded and signed for by the authorising person. Standing orders should be handled in the same way so that they can be reconsidered and changed if business decreases or other factors change.

Part delivery procedure

On acceptance of a part delivery the receiver should record the items received on a part delivery advice form. A copy of this should be attached to the delivery note and handled as a normal delivery note. Another copy of the part delivery advice should be filled with the original purchase order until the completion of delivery.

In the case of standing orders a receiving note should be completed, attached to the delivery note and forwarded to the control officer and subsequently to the bought ledger.

PART DELIVERY ADVICE

175

Supplier A FIRM .... Purchase order ref: 293 ....

.... Date: 14.11.79 ....

.... Delivery note no ....

ITEM OR CODE NO	DESCRIPTION	QUANTITY	UNIT PRICE PER		AMOUNT
N/L	ORANGE JUICE	25	26.25	4x4	£733.25
			TOTAL		£733.25

BALANCE DELIVERY DATE ADVICE .23.11.79...

Order forms

WET STOCK ORDER FORM

Date : 8 10 79 Page :

CODE	DESCRIPTION	UNIT	STORES	CHEFS ORDERS	QUOTATIONS A	B	C	NAME OF SUPPLIER
10	Veal & Ham Pie	lb	3					
12	Salami	lb	1					
21	Honey Cured Ham	lb	-	22	1.45		1.38	Supplier A

Approved : (Chef) Prepared : (Purchasing)

The daily requirements of certain wet stock items will be requested by the Head Chef on a preprinted wet stock order form. In the example above, the Purchasing Clerk has indicated in advance that there is still a stock of veal and ham pies and salami in the stores fridge. The Head Chef's request on this day was for 22lbs of honey cured ham for which the Purchasing Clerk obtained two prices. His decision to purchase the more expensive ham was based on a test comparison the Chef had made a few weeks earlier between all three suppliers. The order form was completed, signed and returned by the Chef to the stores and the order placed. On arrival the ham was weighed, the delivery note verified by the storeman's signature, attached to the wet stock order form and sent to the kitchen for inspection and verification. The delivery note was signed again by the receiver in the kitchen. At a later stage the twice-signed delivery note was collected and recorded in the Goods Received Book.

In the case of dry stock items a firm quote over a long period was obtained from a supplier. In line with an established stock re-order level and order size, the order was placed after the Manager's approval. On arrival the delivery note was attached to the order form, compared, signed and the goods put into the store. After having entered the received quantity on the relevant bin cards, the delivery note was signed again and returned to the Receiving Office. This ensured that the delivery has actually gone into the stores after being received onto the premises.

DRY STOCK ORDER FORM

To

Purchase order NO 3760

Date : 9.10.79

CODE	DESCRIPTION	QTY	UNIT	UNIT COST	VALUE
17A	Honey Portions	50	1x200	5.60	283.00

Delivery date 14 10 79

Time : 15.30

Authorised by :

Cellar orders

The same procedure applies to all cellar orders.

CELLAR ORDER

To:

Purchase order NO 79215

Date : 9 1 79

CODE	DESCRIPTION	QTY	UNIT	UNIT COST £	UNIT COST p	VALUE £	VALUE p
	Courvoisier XXX	2	doz	67	08	134	16
	Bacardi Rum 40 ozs	2	doz	77	90	155	80
	Smirnoff Vodka	2	doz	45	80	91	60
	Beefeater Gin	2	doz	46	58	93	16
	Apricot Brandy	3	bott	44	53	11	13
	Tia Maria	3	bott	50	12	12	54
	Campari	1	doz	42	50	42	50
	Char St Vincent ½ Bottle	2	doz	24	50	24	50
	Macon Rouge ½ Bottle	2	doz	22	60	22	60
	Bulls Blood	1	doz	15	61	15	61
						603	60
				VAT		48	29
				TOTAL		£657	89

Delivery Date : 24 1 79

Time : 1500

Authorised by :

4 Receiving

Receiving procedures

There is little point in setting up specifications for goods or negotiating prices and qualities with suppliers if there is an inadequate system of checking when the goods arrive. It is imperative that all goods enter the premises through a receiving bay and a delivery should only be accepted on the authority of a receiving clerk or someone else with this responsibility.

The receiving clerk should have a copy of the original purchase order so that the incoming goods can be checked against it to ensure that what has arrived is what was actually ordered and so that all sub-standard items can be returned with a note of shortages and returns on a delivery note. Any alteration to the delivery note must be countersigned by the delivery man. If the supplier does not suply a delivery note for some reason, the delivery man should be asked to sign a dummy delivery note which can be drawn up. Suppliers should be encouraged to send priced delivery notes or copy invoices with deliveries so that the actual price can be checked against the agreed price on the purchase order form.

When the goods arrive the copy of the delivery note must be signed and the goods put into the store or cellar and entered on bin cards. If the goods are delivered directly to the kitchen, the Head Chef or Sous Chef must countersign to verify that they have received the goods. This is the one way to ensure that the goods have actually gone into the store, cellar or kitchen. If the receiving clerk has not got the product knowledge necessary to check the quality of wet stock items, the Head Chef should take over the task of physical checking.

At any time during and after receiving goods, and during the handling and entering of delivery notes, errors of various kinds may be discovered. These should be recorded instantly. The supplier should be notified and a correction attached to the delivery note (see page 10). The following steps should be taken when errors arise:

1 The document shown on page 10 is sent to the Stores.
2 Stores notify the supplier and ask for a credit note to be issued immediately.
3 Stores should notify Bought Ledger.
4 Bought Ledger awaits the credit and allows it.

ERROR ON DELIVERY NOTE

SUPPLIER	DELIVERY NO	DATE
F	2001	16.10.79

DETAILS :

£2.00 overcharge on fruit.

TOTAL CREDIT DUE £2.00

Supplier F overcharged by £2.00 on fruit on Wednesday, 10 October 1983. The receiver notified the supplier of this and was promised a credit-note for £2.00 for the next day. If you look at the Goods Received sheet for Thursday, 11 October 1983 (on page 11) you will see that Supplier F has rectified the error by sending a credit note for £2.00 (delivery note number 2032).

All deliveries received must be recorded daily in a goods received or goods inward book for each of the following types of purchases:

1 Food.
2 Beverages and tobacco. This would include a record or containers or empties received and returned.
3 Non-food and beverage items.

A copy of this should be kept in the stores or cellar office.

The originals of all food and beverage delivery notes will be passed to the Food and Beverage Controller and then, finally, to the Bought Ledger where all invoices will be married up with the purchase order form and delivery notes. They should be checked again for the following points:

1 Ensure that the delivery note and invoice have been properly signed by the Receiving Clerk and others.
2 Check the delivery note and invoice against the purchase order, particularly for price.
3 Verify that the purchase order is correctly authorised.
4 Check that the goods received book has been correctly completed from the delivery note or invoice.
6 Check the goods received book for arithmetical accuracy.
7 Check that food has been correctly allocated between that which went direct to the kitchen and that which went into stores.
8 File delivery notes, invoices and purchase orders by supplier.
9 When statements are received from suppliers, check these against the appropriate invoices and delivery notes and pass to the Accounts Department.

10 At the close of each accounting period a schedule should be made of all outstanding delivery notes or invoices for which no statement has been received. This list should be sent to the Accounts Department.

The goods inwards book for food items

The goods inwards book categorises all food purchases as follows:

1 Dry goods.
2 Meat.
3 Fish.
4 Poultry.
5 Fruit and vegetables. Directly delivered to kitchen.
6 Dairy produce.
7 Bread

Below is an example of one day's entries (11 January 1982) of dry goods and wet stock items:
Later you will be able to see how these delivery notes of wet-stock items are broken down on a daily basis into individual commodities in order to obtain easily the individual usage of each commodity after stocktaking. You will also see how one can compare amounts actually used with the potential trading analysis for that week.

The goods inwards book for beverage items

The beverage book can also be categorised under headings, but this is not always necessary. The example on page 13 gives information on daily deliveries, a container received/returned record and an up-to-date balance figure.

GOODS RECEIVED SHEET – FOOD

SUPPLIER	DELIVERY NOTE No.	COMMODITY ANALYSIS								V.A.T.	TOTAL
		DRY STORES	WET STOCK								
			MEAT	FISH	POULTRY	FRUIT/VEG	DAIRY	BREAD	Sub Total Wet Stock		
A	557875							48 57	48 57		48 57
A	557716							3 94	3 94		3 94
A	558011							6 49	6 49		6 49
B	25910							15 28	15 28		15 28
C	474751							30 00	30 00		30 00
D	-							11 40	11 40		11 40
E	-						70 89		70 89		70 89
F	2032					(2.00)			(2 00)		(2 00)
G						72.73			72 73		72 73
H	11134					28.66			28 66		28 66
I	475370					238.68			238 68		238 68
J	84317				38.88				38 88		38 88
K	027255			83.23					83 23		83 23
L	3059			8.00					8 00		8 00
M	60627		156.77		60.80				217 57		217 57
N	041839		161.86						161 86		161 86
O	1425	749.70									749 70
P	11115	360.10								2 98	363 08
		1109.80	318.63	91.23	99.68	338.07	70 89	115 68	1034 18	2 98	2146 96

Further points

1 Priority should be given to the security of store keys. Only a limited number of people should be allowed to enter the stores and the keys should be kept in a secure place. They should be signed in and out every time they are used, even by authorised personnel.

2 Regular delivery times should be established with staff and suppliers to ensure that staff are on hand to take deliveries properly.

3 No unauthorised person should have access to the store or cellar area. The stores must always be locked when the storeman is not present. Beware of helpful draymen or deliverymen. It is quite possible that goods which have seemingly been delivered and signed for can find their way back onto the delivery van rather than into the store.

LIQUOR & CIGARS GOODS RECEIVED SHEET:

DAY: DATE:

DEL NO:	SUPPLIERS:	DESCRIPTION:	UNIT:	AMOUNT:	U/COST:	LIQUOR VALUE:	VALUE OF CONTAINERS REC:		RET:		BALANCE:
47685	CANADA DRY	TONIC WATER	DOZ	115	66½	£76.47½	£86	75	(122	(10)	2084.71
107844	COURAGES	HARP LAGER ½ PINTS	DOZ	100	£1.37	£137.00	£95	00	(85.	(50)	

BALANCE C/F 2058.86

PREPARED BY: CHECKED BY:

5 Storage and requisitioning

The store or cellar should be well laid out, clean and tidy, have sufficient space and be equipped with good shelving which allows easy identification of every stock item. A store organised in this way will minimise the possibility of stock loss.

An adequate control record system should be used. Preprinted index cards for each stock item are ideal. They should show the amount received or issued and stock balances, preferably in quantity and value.

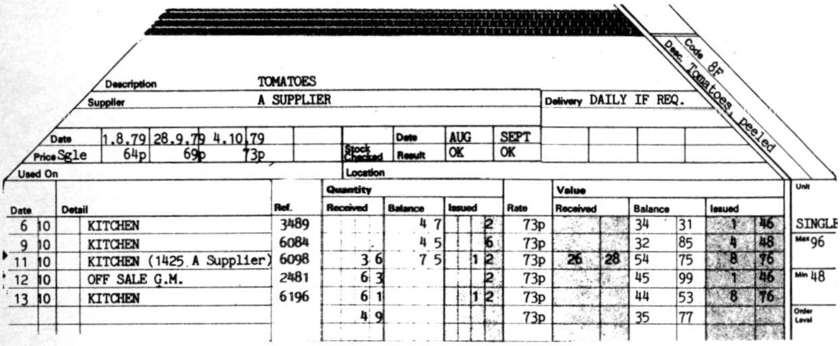
Code 8F
Desc. Tomatoes, peeled
Description TOMATOES
Supplier A SUPPLIER
Delivery DAILY IF REQ.

Date	1.8.79	28.9.79	4.10.79		Stock Checked Date	AUG	SEPT
Price Sgle	64p	69p	73p		Result	OK	OK

Used On
Location

Date		Detail	Ref.	Quantity Received	Quantity Balance	Quantity Issued	Rate	Value Received	Value Balance	Value Issued	Unit
6	10	KITCHEN	3489		47	2	73p		34 31	1 46	SINGLE
9	10	KITCHEN	6084		45	6	73p		32 85	4 48	Max 96
11	10	KITCHEN (1425 A Supplier)	6098	36	75	12	73p	26 28	54 75	8 76	
12	10	OFF SALE G.M.	2481	63		2	73p		45 99	1 46	Min 48
13	10	KITCHEN	6196	61		12	73p		44 53	8 76	
				49			73p		35 77		Order Level

It can be seen from this stock index that one can cost the stock issued on a first in, first out basis. It is, though, preferable to use the latest delivery price when doing the weekly food and beverage cost analysis. This is very useful as a warning indicator. It gives more time to react to cost changes and allows enough time to review menu compositions and gives time to reprint menus or bar tariffs, if necessary, to counteract the actual cost changes that are imminent. If this system is applied the physical stocktaking at the end of the month should, of course, exceed the book value of stocks. The accounts result should never show a higher stock value than the cumulated weekly physical stocktake result. On the contrary, it is usually slightly below this result. The relationship depends very much on stockholding. The more of a commodity held in stock, the longer it will take for current price increases to be reflected in usage.

The storage of beverages

The storage of all products must be carefully thought out. It is a good idea to describe for each item where, and at what temperature, it should be stored. Every staff member should be aware of these facts and regular checks should be made on storage temperatures to prevent spoilage. For beverages, the cellar temperature should vary as little as possible and, if possible, the area should be divided to allow the ideal storage temperature for each type of drink:

1 A wine cellar for red wines at about 56°F.
2 A cooled wine cellar for white, rose and Champagne wines.
3 A cooled cellar for beers.
4 A soft drink cellar.
5 A spirits and liqueurs cellar.

Other points to be borne in mind apart from temperature, are:

1 Rotate stock; first in, first out.
2 Wines should be laid down.
3 Spirits and liqueurs should not be laid down but kept upright.
4 Port and Sherry may be kept upright if they are to be sold fairly quickly.
5 Crusted or vintage Port must be binned or moved with the whitewash mark uppermost.
6 Keep separate bin cards for the same wine of different vintages.
7 Keep a record of breakages with the appropriate evidence.
8 Unwrap all bottles, if in packages, and destroy the packaging. Otherwise a stocktaker can mistake an empty package for a full bottle.
9 Make sure that access to the cellar is controlled.
10 Priority should be given to the security of keys. The keys should be kept in a secure place and signed in and out by the authorised users.

The storage of wet and dry stock

Many of the problems related to the storage of stock are caused by ignorance. It is vital that storage is organised properly and constantly checked. Much information is available from your local health authority and Environmental Health Officers are only too pleased to help in educating staff in these matters.

In large food processing and food handling units an ionization system is a very useful aid. This is used in meat cool rooms and mixed food chillers where it can reduce the bacteria count by more than eighty per cent at an operating temperature of 3°C and at up to ninety per cent humidity. The main benefits of this system are:

1 A reduction in the weight loss of meat in cold storage.
2 Preservation of flavour of stored items.
3 Cross-contamination of flavours is eliminated.
4 Odours in the cold store are eliminated.

5 Bacterial cross-contamination between existing stock and newly delivered meat is very much reduced.
6 The shelf life of goods is increased because of the reduction of the numbers of bacteria in the store.
7 Vitamin content is preserved.
8 Salads and vegetables are kept crisp.

Stores and cellar ledgers

One of the best ways of recording and controlling dry stock and beverage items is a stores and cellar ledger. Here each individual item's usage and stock is recorded daily. The entries should incorporate the following information.

1 The name of the product.
2 The size of the unit.
3 Price and date.
4 Delivery advice.
5 Code number of the product.
6 Date of issue.
7 Name of department to which it is issued.
8 Reference number of department.
9 Quantity and value of deliveries, stocks (balance) and issues.
10 The unit cost rate.
11 Other information, eg:
   a) supplier's name, address and telephone number.
   b) stockholding – maximum, minimum and re-order level.
   c) past price records.
   d) stocktaking discrepancies.

The stores stock, the balance, can be checked by physical stocktaking each day or less often as thought to be necessary. Any discrepancy should be investigated immediately by referring back to bin cards,

A WHISKY 40 oz

DATE	IN	ONE	TWO	THREE	FOUR	FIVE	TOTAL	BAL
	FORWARD							92
24/11/78		12		2			14	78
25/11					1		1	77
27/11				2			2	75
28/11			6		1		7	68
29/11				3			3	65
1/12		6		2			8	57
4/12		6	12		1		19	38
5/12		6		6			12	26
6/12	120						120	146
6/12		12					12	134
7/12		12	6		1		19	115
								115

requisitions and delivery notes. Very often discrepancies are found to be arithmetical errors only. A beverage ledger can be kept in the same way but each item need only be recorded by quantity. The following information should be recorded. i) product name, ii) size of unit, iii) date, iv) deliveries, v) stock, vi) requisitions, vii) names of requisitioning departments. It is essential to record by brand name, such as 'Gordons Gin', and not just 'gin'.

Issuing and requisitioning

Accurate requisition procedures should govern the issue of goods from the stores or cellar. Special times for issuing should be established and made known to all departments. These times should not coincide with delivery times. Emergency procedures should also be established for any requirements after the store or cellar is closed.

Those who are collecting a requisition should not be allowed into the stores or cellar area. Any issues should be recorded in triplicate. Two copies are kept by the storeman and the other copy be given to the requisitioning department. The use of a different coloured requisition form for each department will help the identification of each department. All food and beverage requisitions should include the following information, at least:

1 Name of item (with internal code and brand name, if any).
2 Quantity.
3 Date.
4 Code number of requisitioning department, if any.
5 Signature of Head of Department.

9849 STORES REQUISITION

DATE 13.10.79

2 0	3 4 6
Dept	Code

Cat. No.	Description	Quantity	Unit	Unit Price	Total Value	
8F	Tomatoes, peeled	12	A10	0.73	8	76
23E	Dill cucumber	1	10lts	2.60	2	60
2A	Orange juice	2	16lts	29.25	58	50
3A	Grapefruit juice	3	16lts	28.58	85	65
					155	51

Authorised Signatory

Requisition only
Issued by:

Received by:

LIQUOR REQUISITION № 2149

DEPARTMENT ______________________ DATE __________

QTY.	ITEM	RECEIVED	ENTERED IN CONTROL LEDGER
1	GORDON'S GIN	1	

SIGNED BARMAN ______________________

CELLARMAN ______________________

N.B. 1) USE EVERY LINE: CROSS OUT THOSE NOT USED.

11) INSERT CARBON PAPER.

It is essential that everybody uses standard issuing units. Bottled beers, for example, might only be ordered in multiples of two dozen bottles. Mineral bottles in units of a case. The actual number in a case can vary from supplier to supplier. Make sure also that the requisitions are made by the appropriate authority such as a head of department or an assistant head of department.

The storeman should make up the order and then sign his two copies of the requisition. He should send one copy to the food and beverage controller and retain the other. While he is issuing the storeman should record on the bin card the following information.

1 Date.
2 Amount taken out.
3 Department to which issued.
4 New stock level.

DATE	RECEIVED	IN	OUT	DEPARTMENT
6.10		47	2	Ki
9.10		45	6	Ki
11.10	36	75	12	Ki
12.10		63	2	Off sales
13.10		61	12	Ki

To prove delivery the head of department should check the delivery and sign the storeman's copy.

6 A case study of a liquor stocktake in a bar and a cellar

In this section we will consider an example of a liquor stocktake. This is, in general, a simpler procedure than a food stocktake and this case study will give an indication of how simply the procedure can be adopted for a single bar outlet.

As we have seen before the calculation of the cost of food and beverage as a percentage of sales income is widely used in the hotel and catering industry as a way of comparing current performance with that of past periods or for comparison with general industry standards. It is however more important to compare the *actual* beverage cost with what the cost *should be*. Few establishments know their potential performance in their food and beverage outlets in the face of constant changes in their sales analysis. Bar stock should be taken regularly, preferably at weekly intervals to coincide with revenue reports. If necessary, stock should be taken daily. It is certainly not advisable to extend the period between stocktakes to a month. If there are no problems in the cellar, however, a monthly stocktake is quite acceptable. With revenue control, stocktaking procedures are the most important element of beverage control. It is, therefore, essential to chose the right man to take stock and to evaluate the results. For my own five bar outlets I have a beverage controller who takes stock every Monday with the head barman or with an assistant. The weekly routine of the beverage controller is as follows.

Beverage stocktaker's weekly routine (37½ hours).

Monday	0730	Enter Saturday's issues on to stocktake sheets.	15 mins
	0745	Stocktake Bar Five (food and beverage).	1 hr 30 mins
	0915	Stocktake Bar One (beverages only).	1 hr 15 mins
	1030	Stocktake Bar Three (beverages only).	30 mins
	1100	Stocktake Bar Two (beverages only).	45 mins
	1145	Stocktake Bar Four (beverages only).	45 mins
	1230	Luncheon break.	30 mins
	1300	Extensions of Bar One calculations to be done first.	2 hr 30 mins
	1530	Finished : one result available.	

Tuesday	0900	Extensions of Bar Four calculations.	1 hr 45 mins
	1045	Extensions of Bar Three calculations.	1 hr 15 mins
	1200	Extensions of Bar Two; start.	30 mins
	1230	Luncheon break.	30 mins
	1300	Extensions of Bar Two; continued.	1 hr 30 mins
	1430	Extensions of Bar Five	1 hr 15 mins
	1545	Extensions of Bar Five (food only).	1 hr 15 mins
	1700	Finished : all results available for Food and Beverage Manager.	
Wednesday	0900	(i) Sort out any problems with bars. (ii) Marry-up invoices (if any) with delivery note and purchase order. (iii) Make necessary changes on stocktake master sheet.	
	1230	Luncheon break. (i) Photocopy all master sheets. (ii) Transfer previous weeks' closing stock to this weeks' opening stock. (iii) Prepare beverage reports from stock sheets, photocopy them. (iv) Originals and stock sheets to be filed away.	
	1700	Finished.	
Thursday	0900	(i) Distribute beverage report. (ii) Get cellar ledger up-to-date, starting previous Saturday, moving on to current week. Deliveries first then issues on a daily basis for Monday, Tuesday and Wednesday. These issues and any returns are then entered on stocktake sheets.	
	1700	Finished (with luncheon break 1230–1300)	
Friday	0900	Deliveries and issues for Thursday to be entered in ledger and on stock sheets. Issues to kitchen to be costed and entered on separate control sheet to be passed to food controller next week with Bar Five food and stock take sheets. Deliveries and issues for Friday to be put in ledger and stock sheets ready for Monday.	
	1700	Finished (with luncheon break 1230–1300)	

Stocktaking procedure

Since decimalisation it is much easier to calculate cost and sales value of open bottles in tenths rather than 'outs'. The beverage control sheet (see pages 27 and 28) can be extended in the number of columns depending on the nature of the business and the beverage controller's needs. The column divisions are as follows:

First column: The fluid ounce content of each bottle must be

	established. This can vary greatly, especially in liqueurs.
Second column:	Outs units. Record how many measures you get out of bottles in the case of spirits, liqueurs or aperitifs. Bottled beers and minerals can be recorded in units of a dozen bottles, draught beers in units of one gallon. Wine, Champagne and other bottles in units of one bottle.
Third column:	The names of items which are collected into groups – aperitifs, rums, ports, etc.
Fourth column:	Opening stock in bottles (if full), in tenths (if open bottles), or dozens, gallons or single units as appropriate.
Fifth column:	This includes seven individual columns, one for each day of the week, in which are recorded issues from the cellar to the bar. If there is any return from the bar to the cellar or a transfer to another bar, the figure should be written in red, circled or bracketed to show a credit.
Sixth column:	Issues for the week are totalled in this column.
Seventh column:	Closing stocktake figures to be entered here.
Eighth column:	Total closing stocktake figures.
Ninth column:	Usage or consumption: this is opening stock plus issues minus closing stock.
Tenth column:	Cost per unit. Cost changes (increases or decreases) can be taken from invoices.
Eleventh column:	Cost of consumption.
Twelfth column:	Cost of consumption for the group of beverages (gins, ports etc).
Thirteenth column:	Retail price per unit (excluding VAT).
Fourteenth column:	Cost as a percentage of revenue for each item.
Fifteenth column:	Potential retail sales based on usage.
Sixteenth column:	Potential retail sales based on the usage of the beverage group.
Seventeenth column:	Potential cost percentage for each group.
Eighteenth column:	Potential sales percentage, per group or item, of total beverage sales.

The various sophisticated cash registers now available can be programmed in the same groups as those on the stock sheets, or by aggregations of these groups, so that potential revenue can be compared with actual revenue for each group. The groupings on the stock sheets illustrated (see page 23) are:

Aperitifs	Brandies
Ports	Liqueurs
Sherries	Champagnes
Gins	Wines
Scotch Whiskies	Waters
Irish Whiskies	Squashes
Rye and Bourbon	Draught beers
Rums	Bottled beers
Vodkas	Miscellaneous

These groups can be condensed to:

1 Champagnes, wines, aperitifs, ports, sherries, cocktails, liqueurs.
2 All spirits.
3 Draught beers, bottled beers.
4 Waters, juices and squashes.

Each bar has its own control sheet unless costs, prices, measures and range of goods are the same in all bars. These sheets should be kept up to date and costs and retail prices should be changed as necessary. To save time, the changes can be made by whiting out the old figures and entering new ones. The sheets can then be photocopied for use.

Stocktaking

Points to remember before stocktaking:

1 Have the opening stocks already entered on all the sheets.
2 Enter all transfers and issues onto the sheets before starting.
3 Take stock whilst the bar is closed.
4 Plan and time the stocktake for every bar.

Points to remember during stocktaking:

1 Check that the closing stock is not greater than the total of issues. If it is then check again and query the excess with the barman.
2 Use a hydrometer to check the purity of a drink.
3 If you are suspicious, test a drink by smelling or tasting it.
4 Make sure that you record figures in the correct column and opposite the correct item.
5 Use a scale to establish the contents of beer kegs (see table of container weights on page 24).
6 Record ullages and breakages.

Some keg sizes and weights.

Type	Size	Empty weight (lbs)	Full weight (lbs)	Contents weight (lbs)	Weight of 1 gallon (lbs)	Weight of 1 gallon (lbs & ozs)
Guiness	9 gal	38	131	93	10.33	10lb 5oz
Murphy	10 gal	19	121	102	10.20	10lb 3oz
Double Diamond	18 gal	53	235	182	10.11	10lb 2oz
Carlsberg	11 gal	43	155	112	10.18	10lb 3oz
Harp	9 gal	40	130	90	10.00	10lb 0oz
Harp	18 gal	50	230	180	10.00	10lb 0oz
Watneys	10 gal	20	120	100	10.00	10lb 0oz
Pepsi	4¹/₈ gal	9	55	46	11.15	11lb 2oz
Lemonade	4¹/₈ gal	9	55	46	11.15	11lb 2oz

After stocktaking:

1 Work systematically through the figures.
2 When multiplying the dozen units of bottles by cost and retail price you can use the following chart to convert the part dozens into decimals.

1	– 0.083	7	– 0.583
2	– 0.167	8	– 0.667
3	– 0.25	9	– 0.75
4	– 0.33	10	– 0.833
5	– 0.417	11	– 0.917
6	– 0.5	12	– 1.0

3 Make sure that ullage is returned to the cellar and credited to the bar.
4 Return any broken bottles to the cellar. If no credit or replacement can be obtained from suppliers, dispose of them.
5 If a result seems to be incorrect, check in the following order to track down and eliminate any errors.

(a) Check opening stocks. Compare line by line to see if the last closing stock was transferred accurately to the new control sheet.
(b) Check all the requisitions in the part week.
(c) Check all dates.
(d) Check all transfers between bars.
(e) Check the total issues column.
(f) Check usage. Be on the look out for unusually high or low usages.
(g) Check arithmetic.
(h) Add up and check the totals columns.

If figures are still not correct:

(a) Check draught beer quantities.
(b) Check spillages, breakages and wastage.
(c) Check for any transfers which may be unrecorded.
(d) Talk to the barman.

(e) Check revenue reports for the week.
(f) Check if all bills (banquets, for example) have been processed up to date.
(g) Check if any beverage revenue has been wrongly accounted for as food revenue.

Procedure for dealing with drinks at cost

There are occasions when beverages are sold to customers or staff at cost. This transaction must be taken account of in stocktaking. How this effects results can be seen by looking at the results for Bar Two for week ending 21 January 1979 (page 38). The stocktake resulted in a potential revenue of £2496.55, but actual revenue was only £1220.52. Total cost was £735.92. Therefore *potential* cost was 29.48% of sales, but *actual* cost was 60.29%. It was, of course, obvious to the beverage controller that something was wrong. He spoke to the head of the unit and found that at a staff function £576.43 of drinks at cost had been served. There was also a bill of £50.00 which remained unpaid.

The following procedure was then applied to obtain the correct potential and actual figures for comparison.

1 Take actual revenue figures from the weekly revenue report.
2 Subtract the amount which refers to goods at cost from these total revenue figures.
3 Analyse how this 'goods at cost' figure is made up. Which groups of beverages are involved – spirits, wines, beers, etc.
4 Using the differing cost percentages for each group, it is possible to calculate how much would have been received for these goods if they had been sold at the usual retail prices.
5 This figure is then added back into total revenue.
6 This adjusted figure can now be used as the total revenue figure to work out notional potential and actual results for the week.

Case study of a complete beverage stocktake

The following pages show a complete set of figures referring to a weekly stocktake of an operation with five bars. The figures are made up of:

1 A complete report from Bar One of a week's trading (pages 27–35).
2 A summary report from Bar One for the same week (page 37).
3 Summary reports from Bars Two, Three, Four and Five for a week's trading (pages 38–41).
4 Total summary report on all five bars on one week's trading (page 42).
5 Accumulated summary reports on all five bars on four week's trading (page 43).
6 An analysis of Bar One on one week's trading (page 44).

7 An analysis of all five bars for the same week (page 45).
8 An analysis of price increase effects on Bar One (page 46).
9 An analysis of price increase effects on all bars (page 47).
10 A record of measure size increases referring to Bar One (page 48).

BEVERAGE CONTROL SHEET   PERIOD X   15/1/79 - 21/1/79

OZS	OUTS	ITEM	STOCK	ISSUES M 15	T 16	W 17	T 18	F 19	S 20	S 21	TOTAL ISSUES	CLOSING STOCK	TOTAL C.STOCK	USAGE	UNIT COST	TOTAL COST	TOTAL GRP COST	RETAIL	IND COST %	TOTAL SALES	TOT. SALES PER GRP	COST PER GRP	SALES
	½	Aperitifs																					
35	14	Cynar	1 1/									1/1	1/		3 05			9 59	31.8				
26.4	10.56	Dubonnet Red	4 2/									4/3	3 4/	8/	1 61	1 29		6 06	26.57	4 85			
26.4	10.56	Dubonnet Dry	1 7/									7/1	1 7/		1 52			6 06	25.08				
26.4	10.56	Martini Dry	2 8/	4							4	1/3	3 1/	3 7/	1 29	4 77		6 06	21.29	22 42			
26.4	10.56	Martini Bianco	4 3/									2/4	4 2/	1/	1 27	13		6 06	20.96	61			
26.4	10.56	Martini Rosso	3 8/				2				2	5/4	4 5/	1 3/	1 27	1 65		6. 06	20.96	7 88			
26.4	10.56	Cinzano Bianco	4 7/				2				2	2/4	4 2/	2 5/	1 33	3 38		6 06	21.95	15 15			
26.4	10.56	Noilly Prat	1 2/									1	1	2/	1 54	31		6 06	25.41	1 21			
26½	10.6	St. Raphael	4/									4/	4/		1 47			6 58	22.64				
26½	10.6	Punt - e - mes	4/									4/	4/		2 17			6 58	32.98				
26⅔	10.67	Ginger wine	1 4/									1/1	1 1/	3/	1 05	32		3 36	31.25	1 01			
	Each	Underberg	11									2	2	9	25	2 25		60	41.67	5 40			
	¼																						
26.4	21.12	Campari	3 7/	2							3	2/4	4 2/	1 5/	3 55	5 33		13 69	25.93	20 54			
26⅔	21.33	Pimms No. 1	1 6/									6/1	1 6/		3 32			13 69	24.25				
24½	19.6	Pernod	2 5/									9/1	1 9/	6/	4 77	2 36		13 61	35.05	8 17			
																	22 24				87 24	25.49	2.41
	½	Ports																					
24.64	9.86	Taylors Ruby	3 9/			2					2	4/4	4 4/	1 5/	1 78	2 67		5. 93	30.02	8 90			
																	2 67				8 90	30.0	0.24
																24 11				96 14			

BEVERAGE CONTROL SHEET

15/1/79 – 21/1/79

OZS	OUTS	ITEM	STOCK	ISSUES M	T	W	T	F	S	S	TOTAL ISSUES	CLOSING STOCK	TOTAL C.STOCK	USAGE	UNIT COST	TOTAL COST	TOTAL GRP COST	RETAIL	IND COST %	TOTAL SALES	TOT. SALES PER GRP	COST PER GRP	SALES
	½	Sherries																					
24.64	9.86	Bristol Cream	3 9/				2				2	8/4	4 8/	1 1/	1 81	1 99		6 39	28.33	7 73			
24.64	9.86	Tio Pepe	4 2/				2				2	9/5	5 9/	3/	2 00	60		6 39	31.3	1 92			
24.64	9.86	San Angelo	2 6/	3							3	6/3	3 6/	2	1 58	3 16		5 93	26.64	11 86			
24.64	9.86	San Carlo													1 58			5 93	26.64				
24.64	9.86	San Dorado	4 4/								–	2.1	3	1 4/	1 58	2 21	7 96	5 93	26.64	8 30	29 81	26.7	.82
26⅔	21.33	Gilbeys Gin	4 9/					3			3	2.2	4	3/9	3 80	14 82		13 82		53 90			
	¼	Gins																					
26⅔	21.33	Beefeater	4 4/				3				3	1.2	3	4 4/	3 88	17 07		13 82	28.08	60 81			
26⅔	21.33	Cork Dry Gin	5 4/					3			3	1 1/5	6 1/	2 3/	3 91	8 99		13 82	28.29	31 79			
26⅔	21.33	Gordons	1 4/	4				4			8	1 5/ 4	5 5/	3 9/	3 91	15 25		13 82	28.29	53 90			
40	32	White Satin	6 6/				6				6	2 4/3	5 4/	7 2/	5 47	39 38		20 74	26.47	149 33			
24.64	19.71	Schlichte	5/								–	5/	5/		4 73								
40	32	Burne and Turner	1									–	–	1	3 73	3.73	99 24	13 82		13 82	363 55	27.3	10.04
	¼	Scotch Whisky																					
26⅔	21.33	Bells	2 6/	4		4					8	7/3	3 7/	6 9/	4 07	28 08		13 82	29.45	95 36			
26⅔	21.33	J & B Rare	2 9/								–	1 9/	1 9/	1	4 23	4 23		13 82	30.61	13 82			
26⅔	21.33	Teachers	4 1/	3				3			6	1 8/4	5 8/	4 3/	4 04	17 37		13 82	29.23	59 43			
26⅔	21.33	White Horse	5 6/					3			3	1 3/ 4	5 3/	3 3/	4 04	13 33		13 82	29.23	45 61			
26⅔	21.33	Cutty Sark	5 9/								–	1 9/ 4	5 9/	–	3 94			13 82	28.51				
26⅔	21.33	Kings Ransom	2 5/								–	1 1/ 1	2 1/	4/	5 87	2 35		15 80	37.15	6 32			
26⅔	21.33	Glenfiddich	4 3/								–	2/3	3 2/	1 1/	5 26	2 79		14 81	35.52	16 29			

BEVERAGE CONTROL SHEET 15/1/79 - 21/1/79

OZS	OUTS	ITEM	STOCK	ISSUES M	T	W	T	F	S	S	TOTAL ISSUES	CLOSING STOCK	TOTAL C.STOCK	USAGE	UNIT COST	TOTAL COST	TOTAL GRP COST	RETAIL	IND COST %	TOTAL SALES	TOT. SALES PER GRP	COST PER GRP	SALES
	¼	Rye & Bour. cont.																					
26.4	21.12	Southern C'Fort	2 5/						1*		1*	2/1	1 2/	3/	6 08	1 82		17 01	35.74	5 10			
																	17 14				47 66	35.96	.32
	¼	Rums																					
26⅔	21.33	Bacardi	3 1/	2				2			4	1 6/3	4 6/	2 5/	4 38	10 95		14 81	29.57	37 03			
26⅔	21.33	Tropicano	3 2/								-	1.1	2	1 2/	3 98	4 78		14 81	26.87	17 77			
26⅔	21.33	Capt. Morgan	5 5/	2							2	1 5/3.1	5 5/	2	4 11	8 22		14 81	27.75	29 62			
																	23 95				84 42	28.37	2.33
	¼	Vodkas																					
40	32	Orloff	7 1/				6				6	7/	7/	12 4/	5 27	65 35		20 74	25.41	257. 18			
26⅔	21.33	Smirnoff	3	4							4	8/2	2 8/	4 2/	3 82	16 04		13 82	27.64	58 04			
																	81 39				315 22	25.82	8.70
	¼	Brandies																					
24	19.2	Hennessy X.O.	6/								-	5/	5/	1/	13 37	1 34		26 67	50.13	2 67			
24	19.2	Cordon Bleu	4/								-	4/	4/		10 87			26 67	40.76				
24	19.2	Courvoisier VSOP		1							1	8/	8/	2/	6 97	1 39		22 22	31.37	4 44			
24	19.2	Hennessy VSOP									-				4 10			22 22	18.54				
24	19.2	Hine VSOP	1 1/					1			1	5/1	1 5/	6/	4 54	2 72		22 22	20.43	13 33			
24	19.2	Martell VSOP	8/					1			1	3/1	1 3/	5/	6 65	3 33		22.22	29.93	11. 11			
24	19.2	Remy Martin	1						2		2	1	2	1	8 01	8 01		22 22	36.05	22 22			
																123 95				458 51			

* Returned to cellar.

BEVERAGE CONTROL SHEET 15/1/79 - 21/1/79

OZS	OUTS	ITEM	STOCK	ISSUES M	T	W	T	F	S	S	TOTAL ISSUES	CLOSING STOCK	TOTAL C.STOCK	USAGE	UNIT COST	TOTAL COST	TOTAL GRP COST	RETAIL	IND COST %	TOTAL SALES	TOT. SALES PER GRP	COST PER GRP	SALES
26⅔	21.33	Glenmorangie	2								–	1 3/	1 3/	7/	5 57	3 90		14 81	37.61	10 37			
26⅔	21.33	Isle of Jura	4 4/								–	2 3/2	4 3/	1/	4 35	44		14 81	29.37	1 48			
40	32	Mackinlays	3 7/	6			6				12	2.2	4	11 7/	5 67	66 34		20 74	27.34	242 66			
26⅔	21.33	Chivas Regal	2								–	7/1	1 7/	3/	6 71	2 01		15 80	42.47	4 74			
26⅔	21.33	J Walker B.L.	2 4/								–	1	1	1 4/	4 67	6 54		15 80	29.56	22 12			
26⅔	21.33	Haig Dimple													5 17			15 80	32.72				
																	150 38				518 20	29.02	14.31
	¼	Irish Whiskey																					
26⅔	21.33	Jameson	4 7/								–	6/2	2 6/	2 1/	4 28	8 99		14 22	30.1	29 86			
26⅔	21.33	John Power	3 7/				2				2	1.3	4	1 7/	4 28	7 28		14 22	30.1	24 17			
26.4	21.12	Paddy	4 1/				2				2	5/1	1 5/	4 6/	4 28	19 69		14 08	30.4	64 77			
26⅔	21.33	Old Bushmills	2 6/								–	1 2/1	2 2/	4/	4 09	1 64		14 22	28.76	5 69			
26⅔	21.33	Black Bush	3 7/				2				2	1 6/2	3 6/	2 1/	4 77	10 02		15 80	30.2	33 18			
																	47 62				157 67	30.2	4.35
	¼	Rye & Bourbon																					
24½	19.6	Jim Beam	1 4/								–	4/1	1 4/	–	4 40			14 16	31.07				
24.6	19.68	Jack Daniels	1 5/					2			2	8/2	2 8/	7/	6 08	4 26		14 58	41.7	10 21			
26⅔	21.33	Canadian Club	4 4/								–	1 1/3	4 1/	3/	4 42	1 33		14 81	29.84	4 44			
26.4	21.12	Old Crow	3 4/					1			1	2.1	3	1 4/	5 21	7 29		14 67	35.51	20 54			
26⅔	21.33	Old Grandad	3 1/					1			1	2 8/1	3 8/	3/	5 41	1 62		14 81	36.53	4 44			
26⅔	21.33	Crown Royal	4 8/								–	8/4	4 8/	–	3 08			14 81	20.8				
26.4	21.12	Seagrams V.O.	2 5/								–	1 3/1	2 3/	2/	4 09	32		14 67	27.88	2 93			
																142 17				481 60			

BEVERAGE CONTROL SHEET 15/1/79 - 21/1/79

OZS	OUTS	ITEM	STOCK	ISSUES M	T	W	T	F	S	S	TOTAL ISSUES	CLOSING STOCK	TOTAL C.STOCK	USAGE	UNIT COST	TOTAL COST	TOTAL GRP COST	RETAIL	IND COST %	TOTAL SALES	TOT. SALES PER GRP	COST PER GRP	SALES
	$\frac{1}{4}$	Brandies Cont.																					
24	19.2	Armagnac	4/								–	4/	4/		4 87			17 42					
24	19.2	Courvoisier XXX	5								–	1.1	2	3	5 59	16 77		17 42	32.1	52 26			
24	19.2	Martell XXX	1								–	–	–	1	5 55	5 55		17 42	31.86	17 42			
24	19.2	Polignac	$3^{8/}$	3							3	$1^{1}/_{1}$	$2^{1/}$	$4^{7/}$	5 38	25 29		17 42	30.88	81 87			
																	64 40				205 32	31.37	5.67
	$\frac{1}{4}$	Liqueurs																					
24.6	19.68	Advocaat	$1^{6/}$								–	$2/_{1}$	$1^{2/}$	4/	2 69	1 08		15 85	16.97	6 34			
25	20	Amaretto	$1^{8/}$								–	$6/_{1}$	$1^{6/}$	2/	4 66	93		16 11	28.93	3 22			
$24\frac{1}{2}$	19.6	Anisiette	3/								–	1/	1/	2/	3 33	77		15 79	24.26	3 16			
24	19.2	Apricot Brandy	4/								–	3/	3/	1/	3 71	37		15 47	23.98	1 55			
$24\frac{2}{3}$	19.7	Aquavite	4/								–	4/	4/		4 70			15 87	30.88				
24.64	19.71	Baileys Irish	$1^{4/}$								–	1	1	4/	3 13	1 25		15 37	19.72	6 35			
23.34	18.67	Benedictine	$1^{5/}$								–	$5/_{1}$	$1^{5/}$		5 59			15 04	37.17				
24.64	19.71	Calvados	7/								–	5/	5/	2/	3 49	70		15 87	21.99	3 17			
$24\frac{1}{2}$	19.6	Chartreuse Grn.	4/								–	4/	4/		6 29			15 79	39.84				
24	19.2	Chartreuse Yel	5/								–	5/	5/		4 19			15 47	27.08				
24	19.2	Cherry Brandy	$1^{9/}$								–	$7/_{1}$	$1^{7/}$	2/	3 20	64		15 47	20.69	3 09			
24	19.2	Cointreau	$1^{7/}$								–	$2/_{1}$	$1^{2/}$	5/	5 29	2 65		15 47	34.2	7 74			
24	19.2	C. de Cacao Dark	$1^{5/}$								–	$5/_{1}$	$1^{5/}$		4 78			15 47	30.9				
24	19.2	C. de Cacao Wht.	$2^{2/}$								–	$1/_{1.1}$	$2^{1/}$	1/	4 78	48		15 47	30.9	1 66			
24	19.2	Cr. de Bananes	$1^{2/}$								–	1	1	2/	4 95	99		15 47	32.0	3 09			
																57 47				190 81			

BEVERAGE CONTROL SHEET 15/1/79 - 21/1/79

OZS	OUTS	ITEM	STOCK	ISSUES M	T	W	T	F	S	S	TOTAL ISSUES	CLOSING STOCK	TOTAL C.STOCK	USAGE	UNIT COST	TOTAL COST	TOTAL GRP COST	RETAIL	IND COST %	TOTAL SALES	TOT. SALES PER GRP	COST PER GRP	SALES
	¼	Liqueurs																					
24.6	19.68	C. de Menthe Gr.	$1^{5/}$								–	$2/_1$	$1^{2/}$	3/	3 67	1 10		15 85	24.42	4 78			
24	19.2	C. de Menthe Wh.	2								–	1.1	2	–	4 70			15 47	30.38				
26	20.8	Curacao Blue	$1^{2/}$								–	$1/_1 1/$	1 2/	–	4 68			16 76	27.92				
24	19.2	Curacao Orange	1								–	9/	9/	1/	3 41	34		15 47	22.04	1 55			
23⅔	18.93	Drambuie	$1^{9/}$								–	$5/_1$	$1^{5/}$	4/	4 30	1 92		15 25	31.48	6 10			
24	19.2	Galliano	$1^{2/}$					1			1	$7/_1$	$1^{7/}$	5/	5 43	2 72		15 47	35.1	7 74			
23.44	18.75	Grand Marnier	$1^{9/}$								–	$7/_1$	$1^{7/}$	2/	6 02	1 20		15 10	39.87	3 02			
24	19.2	Irish Coffee Liq	$1^{7/}$								–	$6/_1$	$1^{6/}$	1/	3 66	37		15 47	23.66	1 55			
24	19.2	Irish Mist	1								–	1	1	–	5 22			15 47	33.74				
24½	19.6	Kahula	$1^{6/}$								–	$4/_1$	$1^{4/}$	2/	3 95	79		15 79	25.02	3 16			
24⅔	19.73	Kirsch	$1^{2/}$								–	$2/_1$	$1^{2/}$	–	8 28			15 89	52.1				
20	16	Kummel	$1^{1/}$								–	$1/_1$	$1^{1/}$	–	4 36			12 89	33.82				
16	12.8	Maraschino	1								–	7/	7/	3/	2 05	62		10 31	28.61	3 09			
24½	19.6	Peach Brandy	2								–	1.1	2	–	2 86			15 79	18.11				
24.64	19.71	Roy. Ir Citron	$1^{3/}$								–	$3/_1$	$1^{3/}$	–	3 39			15 87	21.36				
17	13.6	Royal Mint Choc	$1^{9/}$								–	$5/_1$	$1^{5/}$	4/	3 13	1 25		10 96	28.56	4 38			
23.	18.4	Sambuca	6/								–	5/	5/	1/	4 93	49		14 82	33.27	1 48			
23	18.4	Strega	$1^{2/}$								–	$2/_1$	$1^{2/}$	–	4 92			14 82	33.2				
26.4	21.12	Tequila	2								–	$2/_1$	$1^{2/}$	8/	4 26	3 41		17 01	26.22	13 61			
24⅔	19.73	Tia Maria	4/								–	1/	1/	3/	4 18	1 25		15 89	26.31	4 77			
24.64	19.71	CR. Mint	1									1	1	–	3 39			15 87	21.36				
																15 46	25 32			55 23	94 49	26.8%	2.61

BEVERAGE CONTROL SHEET 15/1/79 - 21/1/79

OZS	OUTS	ITEM	STOCK	ISSUES M	T	W	T	F	S	S	TOTAL ISSUES	CLOSING STOCK	TOTAL C.STOCK	USAGE	UNIT COST	TOTAL COST	TOTAL GRP COST	RETAIL	IND COST %	TOTAL SALES	TOT. SALES PER GRP	COST PER GRP	SALES
		Wines																					
	B	Mercier	1		3*				3			2.1	3	4	3 37	14 96		10 19	36.7	40 76			
	½	Mercier	4								–	3	3	1	2 07	2 07		5 56	37.23	5 56			
	B	Paul Perrier							3		3	1.2	3		3 29			7 41	44.4				
	B	Bel Air Claret	6								–	6	6		1 23			3 89	31.62				
	B	Senators	5								–	5	5		1 25			3 89	32.13				
	B	Rose de Prov.	1								–			1	1 48	1 48		3 89	38.05	3 89			
	B	Regina Riesling	10	12							12	4.1.12	17	5	1 00	5 00		2 78	35.97	13 90			
	B	Santa Maria Red	10								–	8/6	6 8/	3 2/	98	3 14		2 78	35.25	8 90			
	B	Santa Maria Rose	4								–	1	1	3	98	2 94		2 78	35.25	8 34			
	½	P. Perrier	3								–	3	3	–	2 88		29 59	5 05			81 35	36.37	2.25
		Draught Beers																					
	Gal	Harp Lager	86	18							18	79	79	25	1 56	39 00		4 00	39.0	100 00			
	Gal	Carlsberg Lager	45	33				44			77	30	30	92	1 43	131 56		4 00	35.75	368 00			
	Gal	Special Bitter	37	40				60			100	47	47	90	1 30	117 00		3 70	35.14	333 00			
	Gal	Guinness	52					45			45	44	44	53	1 77	93 81		4 00	44.25	212 00			
	Gal	Murphy	28					20			20	38	38	10	1 88	18 80		4 00	47.00	40 00			
		Bottled Beers															400 17				1053 00	38.00	29.07
	Doz.	Carling B/Label	6 8/								–	1 1/4 4/	5 5/	1 3/	1 18	1 48		4 44	26.58	5 55			
	Doz.	Carlsberg	4 10/4								4	8/6 7/	7 3/	1 7/	1 29	2 04		4 44	29.05	7 03			
	Doz.	Cider	3								–	4/2 1/	2 5/	7/	1 73	1 01		3 56		2 08			
																434 29				1149 01			

* Returned to cellar.

BEVERAGE CONTROL SHEET 15/1/79 – 21/1/79

OZS	OUTS	ITEM	STOCK	ISSUES M	T	W	T	F	S	S	TOTAL ISSUES	CLOSING STOCK	TOTAL C.STOCK	USAGE	UNIT COST	TOTAL COST	TOTAL GRP COST	RETAIL	IND COST %	TOTAL SALES	TOT. SALES PER GRP	COST PER GRP	SALES
		Bot. Beer Contd.									6	5	6/										
	Doz.	Dopple Bock	$5^{9/}$								–	$7/4/_4{}^{9/}$	$5^{8/}$	1/	3 70	31		8 33	44.42	69			
	Doz.	Heineken	$1^{8/}$	4							4	$3/_3{}^{3/}$	$3^{6/}$	$2^{2/}$	1 33	2 88		4 44	29.75	9 62			
	Doz.	Harp	6								–	$1^{1/}{}_4{}^{2/}$	$5^{3/}$	9/	1 37	1 03		4 44	30.86	3 33			
	Doz.	Guinness	$10^{2/}$								–	$1^{9/}{}_7$	$8^{7/}$	$1^{5/}$	1 45	2 06		4 44	32.66	6 29			
	Doz.	Lowenbrau	$5^{3/}$								–	$2/6/_1{}^{7/}$	$2^{3/}$	3	3 50	10 50		8 89	39.37	26 67			
	Doz.	Pils (Holsten)	$3^{5/}$								–	$5/_2$ 1/	$2^{6/}$	11/	2 28	2 09		7 22	31.58	6 62			
	Doz.	Pale Ale	$2^{3/}$	2							2	$3/_1{}^{11/}$	$2^{2/}$	$2^{1/}$	1 17	2 44		4 44	26.35	9 25			
	Doz.	Foster Cans	$7^{3/}$								–	$4/5/1/_5$	$6^{4/}$	11/	2 90	2 66		7 22	40.17	6 62			
	Doz.	Carlsberg Hof.	$1^{3/}$								–	$1^{2/1/}$	$1^{3/}$		1 48			4 44	33.33				
	Doz.	Carlsberg 68	$1^{4/}$								–	7/	7/	7/	3 09	1 80		8 89	34.76	5 18			
																	30 30				88 93	34.07	2.46
		Waters																					
	Doz.	Mineral Babies	$104^{8/}$	16				248			264	$254^{6/}$	$254^{6/}$	$114^{2/}$	57	65 08		2 11	27.01	240 89			
	Doz.	Juices	$31^{6/}$	12				78			90	$84^{5/}$	$84^{5/}$	$37^{1/}$	91	33 75		3 33	27.33	123 49			
	Doz.	7 – Up	$25^{2/}$					20			20	$39^{2/}$	$39^{2/}$	6	62	3 72		3 33	18.62	19 98			
	Doz.	Pepsi Cola	$4^{11/}$	15				30		3*	42	$27^{6/}$	$27^{6/}$	$19^{5/}$	62	12 04		3 33	18.62	64 66			
	Doz.	Pepsi Draught	$4^{5/8}$					$8\frac{1}{4}$			$8\frac{1}{4}$	$11^{7/8}$	$11^{7/8}$	1	1 19	1 19		5 92	20.1	5 92			
	Doz.	Perrier Water	$3^{11/}$								–	$3^{7/}$	$3^{7/}$	4/	1 84	61		6 67	27.59	2 22			
	Doz.	Vichy Water	11/								–	7/	7/	4/	1 91	64		6 67	28.64	2 22			
	Doz.	Babycham	$1^{8/}$								–	$1^{8/}$	$1^{8/}$	–	1 65			5 00	33.0				
																	117 03				459 38	25.48	12.68
																142 80				548 31			

* Returned to cellar.

BEVERAGE CONTROL SHEET 15/1/79 - 21/1/79

OZS	OUTS	ITEM	STOCK	ISSUES M	T	W	T	F	S	S	TOTAL ISSUES	CLOSING STOCK	TOTAL C.STOCK	USAGE	UNIT COST	TOTAL COST	TOTAL GRP COST	RETAIL	IND COST %	TOTAL SALES	TOT. SALES PER GRP	COST PER GRP	SALES
		Squashes																					
	B	Blackcurrant	1 9/								–	6/1	1 6/	3/	24	07		2 81	8.54	84			
	B	Lemon	4 9/								–	6/2/4	4 8/	1/	24	02		2 81	8.54	28			
	B	Lime	9 8/				12				12	3/14	14 3/	7 5/	24	1 80		2 81	8.54	21 08			
	B	Orange	4 9/									1 1/3	4 1/	8/	24	19		2 81	8.54	2 25			
	B	Peppermint	3 7/									1 5/2	3 5/	2/	21	04		2 81	7.47	56			
	B	Grenadine	7 1/									4/6	6 4/	7/	82	57		2 81	29.18	1 97			
	B	Gomme Syrup													1 11			2 81	39.5				
																	2 69				26 98	9.97	.74

Bar one

Minerals	$13^{6/}$, $9^{4/}$, 11^{10}, $7^{3/}$, 13, $31^{7/}$4, 52, 112	$254^{6/}$
Juices	$11^{1/}$, $5^{2/}$, $14^{2/}$, 54	$84^{5/}$
7 Up	$3^{3/}$, $1^{7/}$, $14^{4/}$, 20	$39^{2/}$
Pepsi	$3^{5/}$, $2^{9/}$, $^{4/}$, 21	$27^{6/}$

Draught beers

Harp (18Gal) 2g, 18g, 54g, 80g, 80g, 70=74g + 2g + 3g	79
Carlsberg (11Gal) 22g, 120, = 22g + 8g	30
Watneys Special (10 Gal) 40g, 90 = 40g + 7g	47
Guinness (9Gal) 90, 70, 36g = 36g + 5g + 3g	44
Murphy (10Gal) 30g, 100 + 30 + 8g	38

Pepsi draught $8\frac{1}{4}$ (50lbs) $8\frac{1}{4}$ + $3\frac{5}{8}$	$11\frac{7}{8}$
Perrier $^{3/}$, $3^{4/}$	$3^{7/}$
Vichy $^{2/}$ $^{5/}$	$^{7/}$
Babycham $^{8/}$1	$1^{8/}$

Potential revenue	£3,622.12	
-breakage + ullage	£ 72.74	
	£3,549.38	
Allowance for drinks sold in C/grill (6%)	£ 5.53	
Final potential revenue	£3,543.85	
Actual revenue	£3,630.80	
+ Bar three transfers	£ 92.18	
+ Bar four transfers	£	
Final actual revenue	£3,722.98	
Variance	£ 179.13	+5.05%
Cost: £1,122.09 + Cost of fruit		£28.68

Bar Three

Transfers	Revenue
	7.05
	28.03
	9.13
	20.22
	9.97
	7.78
	10.00
Total	92.18

Potential Cost%

31.53	Excl. Fruit
32.34	Incl. Fruit

Actual Cost %

30.14	Excl. Fruit
30.91	Incl. Fruit

Final cost £1,150.77

Beverage Report Bar One Week 15.1. - 21.1.79

	Potential		Actual		Variances	
Revenue	£3,543.85	100.00%	£3,722.98	100.00%	+ 179.13	+ 5.05
Cost	£1,150.77	32.47%	£1,150.77	30.91%		- 1.56%
Gross Profit	£2,393.08	67.53%	£2,572.21	69.09%	+ 179.13	+ 1.56%

Potential revenue	£3,622.12	Actual revenue	£3,630.80	Cost	£1,122.09
-breakage and ullage	£ 72.74	+ bar three transfers	92.18	+fruit	£ 28.68
	£3,549.38	Final actual rev	£3,722.98	Total cost	£1,150.77
Allowance for drink sold in bar three	5.53				
Final potential revenue	£3,543.85				

Exclusive of fruit, cost % would be: 31.66 potential, 30.14 actual

Beverage Report   Bar Two   week 15.1. - 21.1.79   Period

	Potential		Actual		Variances	
Revenue	£2,496.55	100.00%	£2,600.78	100.00%	+ £104.23	+ 4.17%
Cost	£ 735.92	29.48%	£ 735.92	28.3%		- 1.18%
Gross Profit	£1,760.63	70.52%	£1,864.86	71.7%	+ £104.23	+ 1.18%
	Actual revenue		£1,220.52		Cost	£732.20
	- drinks at cost		£ 576.43		+ fruit	£ 3.72
			£ 644.09		Total cost	£735.92
	Est. revenue for + above cost factor		£2,006.69			
			£2,650.78			
	Bill not paid last week		£ 50.00	Exclusive of fruit, cost % would be: 29.33 potential 28.15 actual		
	Final actual revenue		£2,600.78			

Refer to procedures for dealing with drinks at cost (page 25).

Beverage Report   Bar Three   Week 15.1. - 21.1.79   Period X

	Potential		Actual		Variances	
Revenue	£870.05	100.00%	£852.07	100.00%	- £17.98	- 2.07%
Cost	£303.21	34.85%	£303.21	35.59%		+ 0.74%
Gross Profit	£566.84	65.15%	£548.86	64.41%	- £17.98	- 0.74%

Potential revenue	£877.81	Actual revenue	£944.25
- breakage + ullage	17.76	- d/bar transfers	£ 92.18
Final potential rev.	£870.05	Final actual rev.	£852.07

Beverage Report   Bar Four   Week 15.1. - 21.1.79   Period X

	Potential		Actual		Variances	
Revenue	£1,980.25	100.00%	£2,104.00	100.00%	+ £123.75	+ 6.25%
Cost	£ 628.54	31.74%	628.54	29.87%		- 1.87%
Gross Profit	£1,351.71	68.26%	£1,475.46	70.13	+£123.75	+ 1.87%
	Actual revenue		£1,010.20 (rest)		Cost	£626.05
			£1,093.80 (bar)		+ fruit	£ 2.49
			£2,104.00		Total cost.	£628.54

Exclusive of fruit, cost% would be 31.61 potential, 29.76 actual

Beverage Report   Bar Five   Week   15.1. - 21.1.79   Period X

	Potential		Actual		Variances	
Revenue	£517.32	100.00%	£520.42	100.00%	+ £3.10	+ 0.6%
Cost	£170.77	33.01%	£170.77	32.81%		- 0.2%
Gross Profit	£346.55	66.99%	£349.65	67.19%	+ £3.10	+ 0.2%

Potential revenue		£534.15
Staff Cola	10.56	
manager's drinks	6.27	£ 16.83
		£517.32

Beverage report All bars 15.1. - 21.1.79 period

	Revenue		Variances		Cost			Sales
	Actual	Potential	£ p	%	£ p	Actual cost %	Potential cost %	Actual %
Bar one	3,722.98	3,543.85	+179.13	+5.05	1,150.77	30.91	32.47	37.99
two	2,600.78	2,496.55	+104.23	+4.17	735.92	28.3	29.48	26.54
three	852.07	870.05	- 17.98	-2.07	303.21	35.59	34.85	8.69
four	2,104.00	1,980.25	+123.75	+6.25	628.54	29.87	31.74	21.47
five	520.42	517.32	+ 3.10	+0.6	170.77	32.81	33.01	5.31
Totals	9,800.25	9,408.02	+362.91	+3.86	2,989.21	30.5	31.77	100%

Beverage Report (All bars) 4 weeks Period 1.1 - 28.1.79

	Potential		Actual		Variances	
Revenue	£42,369	100.00%	£43,645	100.00%	+ £1,276	+ 3.01
Cost	£13,639	*32.19%	£13.639	*31.25%	--------	- 0.94
Gross Profit	£28,730	67.81	£30,006	68.75%	+ £1,276	+ 0.94

* Excluding £171 fruit, cost percentage would be: 31.79 potential, 30.86 actual

Record of group potential returns (potential) Bar one 15.1. - 21.1.79 Period

Group items	Total group cost	Total sales group	Cost % group	Sales %
Aperitifs	£ 22.24	£ 87.24	25.49%	2.41%
Ports	2.67	8.90	30.0%	0.24%
Sherries	7.96	29.81	26.7%	0.82%
Gins	99.24	363.55	27.3%	10.04%
Scotch whiskies	150.38	518.20	29.02%	14.31%
Irish whiskies	47.62	157.67	30.2%	4.35%
Rye and Bourbon	17.14	47.66	35.96%	1.32%
Rums	23.95	84.42	28.37%	2.33%
Vodkas	81.39	315.22	25.82%	8.70%
Brandies	64.40	205.32	31.37%	5.67%
Liqueurs	25.32	94.49	26.8%	2.61%
Wines	29.59	81.35	36.37%	2.25%
Draught beers	400.17	1053.00	38.0%	29.07%
Bottles beers	3.30	88.93	34.07%	2.46%
Waters, juices	117.03	459.38	25.48%	12.68%
Squashes	2.69	26.98	9.97%	0.74%
	£1122.09	*£3622.12	30.98%	100%

* Allowances not yet deducted

Record of group returns (potential) All bars (In this case five bar outlets) week 15.1.79 to 21.1.79

Group items	Total group cost	Total sales group	Cost % group	Sales %
Aperitifs	£ 78.20	314.25	24.88%	3.34
Ports	4.72	11.95	39.5%	0.13
Sherries	23.22	88.03	26.38%	0.93
Gins	208.55	766.29	27.21%	8.14
Scotch whiskies	338.46	1155.97	29.28%	12.29
Irish whiskies	81.83	270.64	30.23%	2.88
Rye and Bourbon	39.77	116.48	34.14%	1.24
Rums	71.57	256.21	27.93%	2.72
Vodkas	184.96	711.47	26.0%	7.56
Brandies	119.29	392.40	30.4%	4.17
Liqueurs	51.08	172.51	29.6%	1.83
Wines	665.27	1844.62	36.06%	19.61
Draught beers	447.72	1170.40	38.25%	12.44
Bottled beers	262.58	855.23	30.7%	9.09
Waters, juices	343.34	1179.55	29.1%	12.54
Squashes	6.82	71.29	9.6	0.76
Cigars	26.94	30.73	12.3%	0.33
Total	2954.32	9408.02	31.4%	100%
Fruit	34.89		31.77%	
Total inc. fruit	2989.21			

Price increase analysis record. Bar one 15.1.79 to 21.1.79

Items	% of sales	% increase	New % of sales based on original revenue
	*	**	
Aperitifs	2.41	49.7%	3.6
Ports	0.24	49.7%	0.36
Sherries	0.82	49.7%	1.23
Gin	10.04	50%	15.06
Whisky	14.31	50%	21.46
Irish whiskey	4.35	50%	6.52
Rye and Bourbon	1.32	50%	1.98
Rum	2.33	50%	3.49
Vodka	8.70	50%	13.05
Brandy	5.67	50%	8.50
Liqueurs	2.61	50%	3.91
Wines	2.25		2.25
Squashes	0.74		0.74
Beers bottled	2.46	2.0%	2.51
Draught beer	29.07	0.5%	29.21
Waters, juices	12.68	5.9%	13.43
Total	100%		127.3

* Figures as per beverage control sheet **page 44**

** Refer to page 48 measure increase record

The new percentage of sale is calculated, in the case of aperitifs, in this way: total new sales as a percentage of old sales, here 149.7% multiplied by the percentage of total sales, here 2.41%, and divided by 100.

Price Increase Analysis Record All Bars 15.1. - 21.1.79

Department	Total Sales	% Increase	New % of Sales based on original revenue
Bar one	37.99	27.3	48.36
two	26.54		26.54
three	8.69		8.69
four	21.47		21.47
five	5.31		5.31
	100%		110.37
	Increase of	10.37%	

Price increase analysis

On page 46 is a budget exercise to assess the effects of measure changes on Bar One turnover. The information in the first column is derived from the weekly stocktake result. The information in the second column from the change of measures and a few price increases.

Measure increases record

Items	Old outs in gills	Fl oz per out	New outs in gills	Fl oz per out	% Increase
Aperitifs	Some 1/6	0.833	1/4	1.25	50
	Others 1/3	1.67	1/2	2.5	49.7
Sherry	1/3	1.67	1/2	2.5	49.7
Ports	1/3	1.67	1/2	2.5	49.7
Gin	1/6	0.833	1/4	1.25	50
Scotches	1/6	0.833	1/4	1.25	50
Rye and Bourbon	1/6	0.833	1/4	1.25	50
Rums	1/6	0.833	1/4	1.25	50
Vodka	1/6	0.833	1/4	1.25	50
Brandies	1/6	0.833	1/4	1.25	50
Liqueurs	1/6	0.833	1/4	1.25	50

It was estimated that an increase in turnover of 27.3% would result if the sales pattern remained the same. The actual increase was 29% because of a change in pattern. The whole exercise took about twenty-five minutes. A further ten minutes work allows us to calculate the effect of this increase on the turnover of all the bars together (see page 47).

What do the figures for Bar One tell us (see page 44)

1 At the end of this week in Bar One, for every £100 spent the cost of sales was £30.98:

$$\frac{£3622.12 \times 30.98}{100} = £1122.09 \text{ cost of sales}$$

2 The highest cost item was draught beer at 38% average cost. It accounted for 29.07% of total sales.

3 If there is an deterioration in overall cost the first item to examine is the sales percentage column. This should be compared with previous weeks in order to determine whether any significant increase of the sales of a particular item has occurred.

We can use this example to show the vital importance of potential cost and sales information. Let us presume that the cost of draught beer remains the same at 38% but that consumption has doubled. Let us also presume that no other decreases or increases in sales have taken place. This would result in a draught beer revenue of £2106 and a cost of £800.34. The total cost for the bar would, therefore, be £1522.26 and the revenue £4675.12. The cost percentage would be 32.56%. This means an overall increase of 1.56% if the usual weekly cost is around 31%. In other words, an increase in costs of £1.56 for every £100 of sales.

In this case, a caterer who did not know his potentials would presume that this cost increase resulted from a mis-handling of money or some other error. Having these potential records available, however, we can compare sales percentage records from one week to another and quickly spot the change. In this case draught beer can quickly be seen to have risen from 29.07% to 45.05% of total sales. This is easy, provided that such information is available. Remember that good management must be based on information.

General comments

A satisfactory liquor result does not necessarily mean that a control system is effective. During my time in catering, I have had dealings with dishonest bar staff in many countries. Whatever the control techniques used, the dedicatedly dishonest barman can often find a way to make extra money. Many barmen are, of course, underpaid and pressured to 'fiddle' to ensure a reasonable income. The most common dishonest practices are these:

1 Under-ringing of purchases and stealing the difference.
2 Not ringing sales up at all and stealing the cash.
3 Overcharging a credit bill customer.
4 Barman bringing in own liquor for sale at bar.
5 Watering down liquor.
6 Short-changing customers.
7 Substitution of cheaper brands of beverages for the usual.
8 Pilferage of stock.
9 Taking drinks while on duty.
10 Giving drinks away.
11 The transfer of bottles to other bars which have different retail prices and, therefore, different potential sales revenues.
12 Fictitious breakages or losses.
13 Short measures.
14 Bring in own soda or minerals.
15 Fictitious off-sales.
16 Recycling products.
17 Poor control of functions where wine or other beverages are inclusive.

To control some of these dishonest practices, there are the following control techniques which are not always enforced.

1 Stocking bars with par stocks.

2 The marking or stamping of bottles.
3 Issuing full bottles only when empty bottles are produced.
4 Use of optics. They should be checked regularly.
5 Lockable optics.
6 Security checks on staff as they arrive and leave.
7 Testing of beverages with a hydrometer to control the watering of drinks.
8 Bar till displayed so that the customer can see the amount rung up.
9 Use of till receipts which must be given to the customers.
10 Use of bar till with an automatic change dispenser.
11 Use of bar till with an automatic drink dispenser.
12 Service staff to pay for drinks before obtaining them from a dispense bar.
13 In the case of wines, replacing what has been sold only.
14 Better control of banquet bars for cash and credit functions.
15 Better control of wine-inclusive functions.
16 Prominent display of bar tariffs.
17 Control of transfers between bars.

The overall liquor result

The ultimate control over the cellar is normally achieved by taking the cellar stock on a monthly basis. This stock-take is used to verify the four weekly bar results. To prepare for this cellar stock-take, another control sheet is needed. This can be based on the bar control sheets. The first column should now be labelled *bin number*. Only two other columns are needed; the eighth column for closing stock and the tenth column for unit costs. The sheet can be folded from the right to cover all the columns to the right of the eighth column (see opposite).

To calculate the necessary figures, closing stock should be multiplied by unit cost and the result can be written on the folded part of the sheet. Each page should be totalled and this total carried forward to the last sheet so that the total value of the cellar inventory is easily calculated.

The same procedure should be followed for each bar outlet to find total stock value.

	Opening Stock		**Closing Stock**	
	£	**Stockholding %**	**£**	**Stockholding %**
Cellar stock	28 402.51	(81.4)	28 964.02	(81.5)
Bar 1 stock	1 453.18	(4.1)	1 357.27	(3.8)
Bar 2 stock	1 434.08	(4.1)	1 487.73	(4.2)
Bar 3 stock	2 113.19	(6.0)	2 071.38	(5.8)
Bar 4 stock	489.07	(1.4)	588.06	(1.7)
Bar 5 stock	1 007.89	(2.9)	1 076.54	(3.0)
	£ 34 899.92	(100%)	£ 35 545.00	(100%)

		Aperitifs															
	B	Angostura											11		1	02	11.22
	B	Cinzano B.											14		1	33	18.62
	B	Martini Dry											196		1	31	256.76
	B	Martini Rosso											135		1	27	171.45
	B	Martini B											31		1	27	39.37
	¼	Brandies Cont.															
24	19.2	Armagnac	4/								–	4/	4/		4	87	£1.95
24	19.2	Courvoisier XXX	5								–	1.1	2	3	5	59	£11.18
24	19.2	Martell XXX	1								–	–	–	1	5	55	----
24	19.2	Polignac	3 8/	3							3	1 1/1	2 1/	4 7/	5	38	£11.30

The purchases during this four week period were £14 107.28. The formula would be:

Opening stock	£ 34 899.92
Plus purchases	14 107.28
	49 007.20
Less closing stock	35 545.00
	13 462.20
Less officers' cheques	250.17
Cost of sales	13 212.03
Actual revenue	£ 41 445.00
% cost of sales	31.88 %

If the monthly report of the beverage controller is compared with monthly cellar results, the results should be the same. In this instance, the costs for each bar were as follows.

	Bar 1	Bar 2	Bar 3	Bar 4	Bar 5	All bars	Fruit
1st week	1376.67	394.61	354.38	554.70	273.57	2953.93	47.80
2nd week	1601.29	730.26	452.06	727.42	235.80	3746.83	47.52
3rd week	1150.77	735.92	303.21	628.54	170.77	2989.21	39.64
4th week	1622.53	677.03	520.65	792.08	336.97	3949.26	35.89
4 weeks	5751.26	2537.82	1630.30	2702.74	1017.11	13639.23*	170.85*

* refer to page 43

Total cost (inclusive of fruit)	£13 639.23
Less cost of fruit	170.85
Liquor cost exclusive of fruit	13 468.38
Less cost of officers' cheques	250.17
	13 218.21

The four-weekly revenue report inclusive of adjustment figures:

Revenue before adjustment	£43 645.00
Less adjustments Bar 2	2 006.69
	41 638.31
Plus cost paid in (Bar 2) see page 38	576.43
	42 214.74
Less officers' cheques	769.74
Actual revenue	£41 445.00
% cost of sales	31.89%

Another quick way to do a comparison is:

Opening stock	£34 899.92
Less closing stock	35 545.00
Difference	645.08
Purchases	14 107.28
Usage/consumption (inc officers' cheques)	13 468.38
Difference	638.90

£13 218.21	from controller's report (pages 51 and 43)	£645.08
13 212.03	accounts result (page 51)	638.90
6.18		6.18

As you can see, both results show the same difference of £6.18.

A plus or minus difference between the two sets of figures can be due to many causes, for example:

1 An error in stock evaluation or counting.
2 Errors in invoices or delivery notes.
3 Changes in purchase prices which were not recorded.
4 Mixing liquor values with container values.
5 Breakages or pilferage.
6 Inefficient stocktaking.

The costing of cocktails

As cocktails increase steadily in popularity it is particularly important to record their standards carefully if costs are to be controlled. The example on page 53 shows the information which should be recorded. Cost should be changed as necessary.
This card can also be used by a barman who is in doubt about the ingredients for a particular cocktail. This is particularly important in an age of ever-changing bar personnel.

However good the control of cocktail costs may be in theory, it is very difficult to enforce the preparation of cocktails according to the standard recipe. If a record is kept of the sales of individual cocktails

RECIPE FOR SINGAPORE GIN SLING CODE No. ☐☐☐☐☐

GLASS "Highball" BAR One

GLASS CONTENT: 12 oz -

UNIT	INGREDIENTS	DATE		DATE		DATE		DATE	
		AT	AMOUNT	AT	AMOUNT	AT	AMOUNT	AT	AMOUNT
1/6 gill	Gin	3.88	0.121						
1/6 gill	Cherry Brandy	3.20	0.108						
1 oz	Lemon Juice	.11	0.018						
1 slice	Lemon	.08	0.010						
7 oz	Soda	.18	0.031						
	Straw		0.005						
	Cocktail stick		0.010						
	TOTAL COST		0.303						
	COST PER PORTION		0.288						

LT/A42

on the cash register, this may help the controller to isolate problems. For example,

1 Six Singapore Gin Slings were sold during a week, according to the cash register record.
2 No Cherry Brandy was sold during the same period as a liqueur on its own.
3 No other cocktail used Cherry Brandy.
4 The stocktake shows (see page 32 of Bar 1 stocktake sheet under *liqueurs*) that the Cherry Brandy usage was two-tenths of the 24.6 fluid ounce bottle, i.e. 4.92 fluid ounces.

The measure of Cherry Brandy used in the cocktail is one-sixth of a gill or 0.83 fluid ounces. The potential usage is then 6×0.83 fluid ounces or 4.98 fluid ounces. The actual usage was 4.92 fluid ounces. Here we can assume that the barman used more or less the correct amount of Cherry Brandy in the cocktail. The exercise shows that one can link fairly accurately a detailed cocktail analysis with cash register and weekly stocktake results. The majority of cocktails contain two or three liqueurs or spirit items. It is, therefore, not unreasonable to expect an under-usage of around 0.06 fluid ounces per ingredient in each cocktail. If the barman is inexperienced this can be an over-usuage.

Bottle and container control

To control bottles and containers a daily record of their receipt and return is needed which is equivalent to the goods received record. This is particularly important when the cost of containers can be more than the cost of their contents. On page 54 is the total record of containers held, received and returned in one day. (see page 13).

Value of containers

Received	Returned	Balance
Balance b/f		£2084.71
£86.75	(£122.10)	
£95.00	(£ 85.50)	
Balance c/f		£2058.86

From page 13 we can see that tonic waters have been delivered. The values of the bottles and containers received or refunded is put into the credit or debit column as necessary and the balance adjusted. The new balance will be carried forward to the next day. The figures relating to the delivery of tonic waters were arrived at as follows. The deposit on bottles is 45 pence per dozen. The deposit on cases is £1 each.

Delivery of 115 dozen with 35 cases
115 × £0.45 = £51.75
35 × £1.00 = £35.00

£86.75 debit

Containers returned – 158 dozen bottles with 51 cases
158 × £0.45 = £71.00
51 × £1.00 = £51.00

£122.10 credit

A monthly stocktake is quite sufficient to find the total value of containers on the premises. This value is then entered on the goods received sheet as the total value of containers bought forward at the beginning of the month. (See also pages 56 and 57 for the closing/opening stock record.) There will always be a variance between actual and potential figures for container values and these are mainly due to breakages and losses. Nevertheless it is important that the controller checks all container credits and debits when he is marrying up invoices with the purchase order and delivery note. As a double control he can itemise containers received in a time period as opposite.

Containers received and returned during the period from 29.4.79 to 28.5.79

	Received			Returned		
	Bottles (Dozens)	Cases	Tanks	Bottles (Dozens)	Cases	Tanks
Canada Dry	115	35	–	158	51	–
Courages	100	50	–	90	45	–
Watneys	50	25	–	52	26	–
Coca Cola	50	25	–	64	37	–
Schweppes	310	80	–	237	68	–
Carlsberg	20	10	–	–	–	–
Canada Dry	158	46	3	125	54	10
Schweppes	150	40	–	156	39	–
Watneys	66	33	–	50	34	–
Coca Cola	100	50	–	96	48	–
Canada Dry	120	35	3	64	18	2
Courages	100	50	–	–	50	–
Schweppes	40	10	–	132	33	–
Coca Cola	60	30	–	66	33	–
Carlsberg	20	10	–	–	–	–
Schweppes	254	66	–	132	63	–
Watneys	90	35	–	–	–	–
Canada Dry	286	82	8	133	38	4
Canada Dry	40	10	–	–	–	–
Courages	60	30	–	60	30	–
Schweppes	350	90	–	156	75	–
Watneys	86	43	–	126	77	–
Coca Cola	100	50	–	8	4	–
Carlsberg	20	10	–	–	–	–
Total	2 745	945	14	1 905	823	16
Coca Cola	310	155	–	234	122	–
Beer	612	296	–	378	262	–
Minerals/Juice /Babychams	1 823	494	14	1 293	439	16
Total	2 745	945	14	1 905	823	16
Value per unit	£0.45	£1.00	£4.00	£0.45	£1.00	£4.00
Total received /returned	1 235.25	945.00	56.00	857.25	823.00	64.00
Grand Total		£2 236.25			£1 744.25	

At the end of the period stock will be taken and these figures should then correspond with the latest brought forward balance on the container report. There are various ways to compare the balance figure of the goods received sheet with the actual stocktake. For example:

Opening Stock (page 13)	£2 084.71	
plus received	£2 236.25	
	£4 320.96	
Minus returned	£1 744.25	
Balance 28.5.79	£2 576.71	as per goods received sheet
Actual stocktake	£2 581.04	See closing stocktake (page 57)
Difference +	£ 4.33	

Or,

Opening Stock	£2 084.71
plus difference between received and returned	£ 492.00
Balance	£2 576.71
Minus actual stocktake	£2 581.04
Difference	£ 4.33

Or, stocktake evaluation by total numbers and total value.

	Bottles		Cases		Tanks	
Balance 30.4.79	$2101\,^{7}/_{12}$	£ 945.71	1027	£ 10.27	28	£112.00
Received	2745	£1235.25	945	£ 945.00	14	£ 56.00
	$4846\,^{7}/_{12}$	£2180.96	1972	£1972.00	42	£168.00
Returned	1905	£ 857.25	823	£ 823.00	16	£ 64.00
Balance 28.5.79	$2941\,^{7}/_{12}$	£1323.71	1149	£1149.00	26	£104.00
Closing stocktake	$2953\,^{5}/_{12}$	£1329.04	1148	£1148.00	26	£104.00
Difference	$+11\,^{10}/_{12}$	+£ 5.33	−1	−£ 1.00	Nil	Nil

Opening Stock

Stocktaking 29.4.79　　Containers (single)　　Period Ending: 29.4.79

	One	Two	Three	Four	Five	Cellar and cage	Total	Cost per unit	Total cost
Minerals, Baby	69	33	10	16	11	259	398	1.00	398.00
Juices	31	7	5	4	4	67	118	1.00	118.00
Coca Cola	7	11	2	2	4	155	181	1.00	181.00
Babycham	1	–	–	1	–	6	8	1.00	8.00
Beers	18	23	12	10	–	259	322	1.00	322.00
Canisters	3	–	4	–	–	21	28	4.00	112.00
									1139.00

Stocktaking 29.4.79 **Bottles (Doz) (Full and Empty)** **Period Ending: 29.4.79**

	One	Two	Three	Four	Five	Cellar and cage	Total	Cost per unit	Total cost
Minerals, Baby	$106^{3}/_{12}$	$80^{1}/_{12}$	17	$60^{4}/_{12}$	$38^{7}/_{12}$	763	$1065^{3}/_{12}$		
Juices	$78^{3}/_{12}$	$16^{3}/_{12}$	$11^{4}/_{12}$	$7^{2}/_{12}$	11	201	325		
Coca Cola	$9^{8}/_{12}$	12	10	$4^{8}/_{12}$	$8^{10}/_{12}$	234	270		
Babycham	2	–	–	2	–	12	16		
Beers	38	$34^{7}/_{12}$	$22^{9}/_{12}$	19	–	311	$425^{4}/_{12}$		
Total							$2101^{7}/_{12}$	45p	945.71
									2084.71

Closing Stock

Stocktaking 28.5.79 **Containers (single)** **Period Ending: 28.5.79**

	One	Two	Three	Four	Five	Cellar and cage	Total	Cost per unit	Total cost
Minerals, Baby	43	8	9	30	9	273	372	1.00	372.00
Juices	24	4	8	10	5	212	263	1.00	263.00
Coca Cola	1	1	2	12	1	128	145	1.00	145.00
Babycham	–	–	1	1	–	6	9	1.00	9.00
Beers	16	7	6	23	–	307	359	1.00	359.00
Canisters	2	4	–	–	–	20	26	4.00	104.00
									1252.00

Stocktaking 28.5.79 **Bottles (Doz) (Full and Empty)** **Period Ending: 28.5.79**

	One	Two	Three	Four	Five	Cellar and cage	Total	Cost per unit	Total cost
Minerals, Baby	$207^{7}/_{12}$	$28^{4}/_{12}$	$42^{1}/_{12}$	$122^{7}/_{12}$	$24^{9}/_{12}$	904	$1329^{3}/_{12}$		
Juices	$76^{8}/_{12}$	$15^{9}/_{12}$	$12^{3}/_{12}$	30	$10^{8}/_{12}$	599	$744^{3}/_{12}$		
Coca Cola	$6^{7}/_{12}$	$1^{8}/_{12}$	$5^{10}{}_{1}/_{2}$	20	$1^{6}/_{12}$	212	$247^{6}/_{12}$		
Babycham	7	–	$2^{3}/_{12}$	$1^{4}/_{12}$	–	12	$16^{2}/_{12}$		
Beers	$34^{4}/_{12}$	$18^{2}/_{12}$	$16^{6}/_{12}$	$39^{3}/_{12}$	–	508	$616^{3}/_{12}$		
Total							$2953^{5}/_{12}$	45p	1329.04
									2581.04

Finally another control is to break down the container and bottle stocktake into certain groups, or if desired an even more detailed breakdown into suppliers and their individual products.

	Bottles	Cases
1 Opening stock Coca Cola	270	181
Received	+ 310	155
	580	336
Returned	− 234	122
	346	214
Closing stock	− $247^{6}/_{12}$	145
Difference	− $98^{6}/_{12}$	−69
2 Opening stock beers	$425^{4}/_{12}$	322
Received	+ 612	296
	$1037^{4}/_{12}$	618
Returned	− 378	262
	$659^{4}/_{12}$	356
Closing stock	$616^{3}/_{12}$	359
Difference	− $43^{1}/_{12}$	+3
3 Opening stock minerals/juices	$1406^{3}/_{12}$	524
Received	+1823	494
	$3229^{3}/_{12}$	1018
Returned	−1293	439
	$1936^{3}/_{12}$	579
Closing stock	−$2089^{8}/_{12}$	644
Difference	+ $153^{5}/_{12}$	+65

	Tanks
4 Opening stock	28
Received	+14
	42
Returned	−16
	26
Closing stock	26
Difference	Nil

5 Summary

	Bottles	Cases
	$-\ 98^{6}/_{12}$	$-\ 69$
	$-\ 43^{1}/_{12}$	$+\ 3$
	$-\ 141^{7}/_{12}$	$-\ 66$
	$+\ 153^{5}/_{12}$	$+\ 65$
Total	$+\ 10^{10}/_{12}$	$+\ 1$

7 Food control: stocktaking

A stocktake of food should be taken at regular intervals – weekly, or if necessary on a daily basis. The stocktake should preferably co-incide with the revenue report. It is not advisable to extend this period to a monthly one because it is very difficult to isolate and control sources of variance if the period between stocktakes is longer than a week. If there are consistently no discrepancies apparent in your stores, a monthly stocktake here is acceptable.

With revenue control, stocktaking procedures are the most important element of food control. It is, therefore, essential to choose the right person to take stock. They must be able to recognise commodities and evaluate the stocktake figures. The amount of time needed depends on the size of the establishment. In the operation discussed in the following pages there are six food and beverage outlets and control is handled by:

1 One beverage controller.
2 One food controller who produces weekly potential results and does all menu costings and prepares statistics.
3 One food controller who is responsible to the Accounts Department rather than to the Food and Beverage Department. He takes the physical stock of all food, both wet and dry stocks goods in the kitchen every Monday morning. He also takes the main stores stock each month.

Control sheets

To aid speed and accuracy a set of stocktake control sheets is needed. In this case three sets are used. One set for wet stock items, one for dry stock, and one for inter-departmental stocktaking. Each set is coded and each is coloured differently for easy recognition. Each sheet is devised so that it can easily be linked with the daily purchases of each food item and the following can easily be established.

1 Total purchases of each individual food item.
2 The average price of the weekly purchases of each food item.
3 Cost decreases or increases on previous week for each item.
4 The opening stock and subsequent purchases of each item.

The column divisions of the stocktake sheets are shown below:

DATE	CODE	CLOSING STOCK	STOCK		USAGE	
COMMODITY		DATE	UNIT	£p	UNIT	£p

Column 1: the name of each commodity.
Column 2: code for each commodity.
Column 3: the actual closing stock of each commodity and the date of the stocktake.
Column 4: the number of units of each commodity and the value of the stock.
Column 5: the total consumption (usage in number of units add value for each food item.)

The column divisions on the sheet of the daily purchases record (opposite) are as follows:

Column 1: Opening stock for each item by unit and value.
Column 2: The names of commodities.
Column 3: Code.
Column 5: Last week's average price.
Columns 6–12: The date, day, usage in units, price per unit, and the total value of purchases for each day.
Column 13: Total of weekly purchases for each item by unit and value with average price per unit.
Columns 14–15: A record of cost decrease or increase during the week.
Column 16: Opening stock plus purchases during the week by unit and value.

The controller should transfer all the previous week's closing stock figures from the stocktake sheet onto the daily purchases analysis sheet. He should also record the previous week's average price on the sheet. After receiving the daily delivery notes he will record all purchases by commodity, unit and value under the appropriate day. At the end of the week, purchases must be totalled by units and value and the average price calculated. If there was a difference in the average price over the previous week, the total number of units is multiplied by the change in unit price and this is entered. The opening stock is then added to purchases.

All these entries should, preferably, be completed before stocktaking because these records should be attached to the stocktake sheets so that any abnormalities can be seen immediately and can be rectified or queried on the spot.

New items produced during the week's production in the kitchen can be coded immediately and credited. Items which were bought last will appear on the stocktake on a *first-in*, *first-out* principle for each commodity item. Any items missed during a previous stocktake must appear as a credit.

Structuring

Special attention must be given to items which were bought on the bone, untrimmed or uncooked and which are found during the stocktake as deboned, trimmed or cooked items, sliced or unsliced. In order

OPENING STOCK		DATE	UNITS	CODE	LAST WEEK AVERAGE	MONDAY			TUESDAY			WEDNESDAY			THURSDAY			FRIDAY			SATURDAY			SUNDAY			WEEKLY			COST		OPENING STOCK PLUS PURCHASES	
UNIT	£p	COMMODITY				UNIT	PRICE	TOTAL	UNIT	PRICE	TOTAL	UNIT	PRICE	TOTAL	UNIT	PRICE	TOTAL	UNIT	PRICE	TOTAL	UNIT	PRICE	TOTAL	UNIT	PRICE	TOTAL	TOTAL PURCHASE UNITS	£p	AVERAGE PRICE	DECREASE	INCREASE	UNIT	£

to value this kind of stock the stocktaker should plan an exercise to record it and value it according to agreed principles which all feel to be fair and accurate. For example,

	Ratio	Gross weight	Cost per lb	Total cost	% increase for stock available
Leg of beef (top piece)	100%	110 lbs	.72	79.20	
Fat	22.73%	25 lbs			
Bones	18.18%	20 lbs			
Meat (raw)	59.09%	65 lbs	1.22		purchase + 69.5%
Cooking loss 25% of net meat		16¼ lbs			
Meat (cooked) 75% of net meat		48¾ lbs	1.62		trimmed raw meat cost + 33%

Instruction to controller for stock evaluation of leg of beef

1 If fat and bones are trimmed off, allow purchase price plus 69.5% increase because of fat and bone loss (which make up 41% of the gross weight.)
2 If the meat is cooked allow 25% of the net (trimmed) weight for shrinkage. Allow net meat price plus 33% price increase.
3 To allow for trimming and cooking together allow purchase price plus 125%.
4 If the meat has been kept in the refrigerator for one week allow 5% weight loss.

Slow roasting can reduce shrinkage by 5% to 20% of total weight. If meat is kept in the refrigerator for more than one week a label showing date of purchase, supplier's name, weight and price should be attached to it. If an operation does its own butchery, a yield test for various cuts should be carried out once a month.

Points to remember before stocktaking

1 Have all control sheets prepared with a record of opening stock.
2 Enter all issues onto the dry goods stocktake sheets.
3 Enter all purchases onto wet goods stocktake sheets.
4 Total issues and purchases for each item and add to opening stock.
5 Make sure that you take stock before any further issue and before any sales take place.
6 Plan and time the stocktake for every unit of the operation.

Points to remember during stocktaking

1 Make sure that you know all the places where stock may be stored.
2 Check that closing stock is not greater than opening stock plus any issues or purchases. If this is so, check again and query the excess with the chef.
3 Always use a scale to establish correct weights.
4 Record everything accurately.

Points to remember after stocktaking

1 Work systematically through any extension calculations line by line.
2 When multiplying units by unit price make sure that you have the correct units and the correct price.
3 Apply the *first in, first out* principle to stock.
4 If any results seem to be incorrect check through in the following order to eliminate errors:
   (a) Check opening stock. See that closing stock from the previous week was transferred without error from sheet to sheet.
   (b) Check all requisitions or purchases and tick them off figure by figure.
   (c) Check the dates of requisitions.
   (d) Check all transfers of stock.
   (e) Check the total issues or purchases column.
   (f) Check usage. Look for unusually high or low usage. Compare figures with those for previous weeks.
   (g) Check all you calculations.
   (h) Check revenue reports.
   (i) Check that all bills (banqueting perhaps) have been put through before the stocktake.
   (j) Check that food revenue was not accounted for as beverage revenue.
   (k) Discuss the problem with the Head Chef.
   (l) Find out if there have been any changes of procedure.
   (m) Compare with potential results if the result still seems unsatisfactory.
   (n) Have all allowances been taken into consideration?

The following are often causes of poor food cost results and should be borne in mind.

1 Overproduction.
2 Menu items which are seldom ordered.
3 The preparation of a dish deviating from the standard recipe.
4 Inconsistent portion sizes.
5 Unusual waste in preparation.
6 Poor trimming.
7 Overcooking.
8 Careless food handling.

9 Employees eating more than their allowance.
10 Pilferage.
11 Spoilage due to poor storage.
12 Poor receiving procedures which allow inaccurate weighing or counting or lack of checks for quality.
13 Over-purchasing.
14 Failure to ensure credit for damaged goods or goods not received.
15 Collusion between receiving and/or accounting employees and suppliers.
16 Insufficiently trained or qualified employees.
17 Pricing errors on customer's bills.
18 Poor control over the recording and collecting of invoices.

8 Case study of a complete food stocktake

The following pages show a complete set of figures and documents referring to a weekly stocktake. The figures are made up of:

1 One week's actual purchase of all wet stock items summarised. (page 68)
2 The same week's dry goods requisitions from stores. (page 70)
3 All these are combined with opening and closing stocks and increases and decreases in actual consumption. (pages 69–71).
4 A summary of cost decreases and increases per group for a week. (page 72)
5 A complete actual food cost result with the following information:
   (a) Daily total wet stock purchases grouped under meat, fish, poultry, fruit and vegetables, dairy produce and bread. These are totalled for the week.
   (b) Daily total issues of all dry stock items as shown on requisitions.
   (c) Daily total liquor requisitions.
   (d) Total gross cost.
   (e) Staff allowances.
   (f) Net costs daily and totalled.
   (g) Actual revenue daily and totalled.
   (h) Food cost percentage for the week.
   (i) Percentage of total purchases and requisitions accounted for by each commodity group.
   (j) Total stock holdings of each group and this expressed as a percentage of total stockholding.
   (k) Total closing stock for each group and this expressed as a percentage of total closing stock.
   (l) Total purchases plus opening stock.
   (m) Total consumption of each group and this expressed as a percentage of total consumption.
   (n) Further allowances such as off-sales (see page 76) and bar allowances. Once the final actual cost is calculated this is compared with total revenue for the week.
   (o) Cost increases and decreases recorded in total and expressed as a percentage of purchases.

OPENING STOCK 8.10.79 UNIT Ep	DATE 8.10.79 COMMODITY	UNITS	CODE	LAST WEEK AVERAGE	MONDAY 8th UNIT	MONDAY PRICE	MONDAY TOTAL	TUESDAY 9th UNIT	TUESDAY PRICE	TUESDAY TOTAL	WEDNESDAY 10th UNIT	WEDNESDAY PRICE	WEDNESDAY TOTAL
3828.95	Meat Summary	(3	Sheets)				1233.01			479.25			1049.52
1053.12	Fish "	(2	Sheets)				138.74			145.83			168.29
519.98	Poultry "	(1	Sheet)				414.06			72.80			11.55
824.87	Fruit/Veg "	(4	Sheets)				233.31			279.84			134.98
1404.69	Dairy "	(4	Sheets)				409.98			320.05			253.79
	Bread Sheet One (Part)												
55.65	Italian Rolls	100	A1	2.65	200	2.65	6.30	200	2.65	5.30	150	2.65	3.98
	Vienna Small	100	A2	2.47	700	2.47	17.29	600	2.47	14.82	580	2.47	14.33
	Baton	100	A3	2.77	650	2.77	18.00	600	2.77	16.62	570	2.77	15.79
	Long Seed	100	A4	2.78	100	2.78	2.78	100	2.78	2.78	100	2.78	2.78
	Baps	Ea.	A5	.07	48	7	3.36	48	7	3.36	48	7	3.36
265.20	Croissant	Doz	A6	.60	67	60	40.20	50	60	30.00	67	60	40.20
29.16	Loaves	Ea.	A7	.27	66	.27	17.82	72	27	19.44	66	.27	17.82
.70	Hovis Sliced	Ea.	A8	.17½	4	17½	.70	4	17½	.70	4	17½	.70
769.00	Summary Sheet	One	Two/Three				124.77			124.98			252.80
8386.61	Summary of All	Sheets					3148.62			1578.35			1815.93

COMMODITY	THURSDAY 11th UNIT	THURSDAY PRICE	THURSDAY TOTAL	FRIDAY 12th UNIT	FRIDAY PRICE	FRIDAY TOTAL	SATURDAY 13th UNIT	SATURDAY PRICE	SATURDAY TOTAL	SUNDAY 14th UNIT	SUNDAY PRICE	SUNDAY TOTAL	WEEKLY TOTAL PURCHASE UNITS	WEEKLY TOTAL PURCHASE Ep	WEEKLY AVERAGE PRICE	COST DECREASE	COST INCREASE	OPENING STOCK PLUS PURCHASES UNIT	OPENING STOCK PLUS PURCHASES £
Meat Summary			318.63			1043.98			172.78			—		4702.77		122.72	148.12		8531.72
Fish "			97.23			381.05			29.70			—		969.84		13.20	25.50		2002.96
Poultry "			99.68			275.16			108.80			—		982.05		22.14	17.52		1502.03
Fruit/Veg "			338.07			261.93			160.73			174.52		1583.38		94.90	134.39		2408.25
Dairy "			70.89			992.02			90.72			83.66		2215.84		24.29	5.64		3620.53
Bread Sheet One (Part)																			
Italian Rolls	150	2.65	3.98	200	2.65	5.30	225	2.65	5.96	100	2.65	2.65	1225	32.47	2.65			33.25	88.12
Vienna Small	650	2.47	16.06	725	2.47	17.91	775	2.47	19.14	600	2.47	14.82	4630	114.37	2.47			46.30	114.37
Baton	550	2.77	15.24	955	2.77	26.45	775	2.77	21.47	600	2.77	16.62	4700	130.21	2.77			47.00	130.21
Long Seed		—		145	2.78	4.03	225	2.78	6.25	50	2.78	1.39	720	20.01	2.78			720	20.01
Baps		—		96	7	6.72	48	7	3.36	48	7	3.36	336	23.52	.07			336	23.52
Croissant	50	60	30.00	67	.60	40.20	59	.60	35.40	59	60	35.40	419	251.40	.60			861	516.60
Loaves	76	.27	20.52	72	.27	19.44	76	.27	20.52	76	.27	20.52	504	136.08	.27			612	165.24
Hovis Sliced	4	17½	.70	4	17½	.70	4	17½	.70	4	17½	.70	28	4.90	17½			32	5.60
Summary Sheet			115.68			198.63			164.36			146.19		1308.06		2.12	4.80		2057.06
Summary of All Sheets			1034.18			3052.77			667.09			405.00		11741.94		279.37	330.97		20122.55

DATE 14.10.79 COMMODITY	CODE	CLOSING STOCK DATE 14.10.79	STOCK UNIT	STOCK £p	USAGE UNIT	USAGE £p
				3161.19		5370.53
				1015.48		987.48
				845.05		656.98
				725.36		1682.89
				1614.07		2006.46
ITALIAN ROLLS	A1		2000	53.00	1325	35.12
VIGNNA SMALL	A2		–	–	4630	114.37
BATON	A3		–	–	4700	130.21
LONG SEED	A4		–	–	720	20.01
BAPS	A5		48	3.36	288	20.16
CROISSANT	A6		442	265.20	419	257.40
LOAVES	A7		88	23.76	524	141.48
HOVIS SLICED	A8		–	–	32	5.60
				839.85		1217.21
				8201.00		11921.55

OPENING STOCK UNIT	OPENING STOCK £p	DATE 8.10.79 COMMODITY	UNITS	CODE	LAST WEEK AVERAGE	MONDAY 8th UNIT	MONDAY PRICE	MONDAY TOTAL	TUESDAY 9th UNIT	TUESDAY PRICE	TUESDAY TOTAL	WEDNESDAY 10th UNIT	WEDNESDAY PRICE	WEDNESDAY TOTAL	THURSDAY 11th UNIT	THURSDAY PRICE	THURSDAY TOTAL	FRIDAY 12th UNIT	FRIDAY PRICE	FRIDAY TOTAL	SATURDAY 13th UNIT	SATURDAY PRICE	SATURDAY TOTAL	SUNDAY 14th UNIT	SUNDAY PRICE	SUNDAY TOTAL	WEEKLY TOTAL PURCHASE UNITS	WEEKLY TOTAL PURCHASE £p	WEEKLY AVERAGE PRICE	COST DECREASE	COST INCREASE	OPENING STOCK PLUS PURCHASES UNIT	OPENING STOCK PLUS PURCHASES £
	363.39	SHEET 1		B				199.06						197.76						131.93								528.75		.38	.24		892.14
	169.89	2		I				13.65			1.56			·.00			26.98			58.78								108.97		3.13	6.64		278.86
	67.67	3		M							10.90			2.78			3.50			7.68								42.86					110.53
	127.28	4		O																								–					127.28
	864.96	5		A				297.73						487.05						270.06			144.05					1198.89			·20		2063.85
	231.86	6		N				40.96			39.64			28.50			58.97			42.92			38.00					248.49		4.81			480.35
	182.48	7		L				13.94			5.40			23.55						19.16			4.44					66.49		·49	7.41		248.97
	67.36	8		K				11.26						·70			1.35											13.25					80.61
	62.02	9		J				8.66						7.15			1.47			1.70								18.98		·34			81.00
	259.27	10		G				66.88			16.02			29.02			37.80			70.98								220.70		5.84	1.62		479.97
	33.06	11		H							10.70						.77			7.30			17.52					36.29					69.35
	138.56	12		F				40.92			19.62						12.20			32.80			8.76					114.30		3.60	11.68		252.86
	350.61	13		E				37.98			34.74			21.62			22.78			68.16			2.60					187.88					538.49
	164.81	14		D							5.75																	5.75					170.56
	77.92	15		C							32.16						6.96											39.12			·96		117.04
	3513.06	TOTAL 1-15						730.48			176.49			824.13			172.78			711.47			215.57	–	–	–		2830.72		12.59	22.75		6343.78
	19.31	SHEET 16		P				14.66						11.99						22.41			10.40			2.60		62.06					81.87
		16A		P				7.04			4.54			7.04			4.54			12.06			4.54			–		39.76					—

DATE / COMMODITY	CODE	CLOSING STOCK DATE 14.10.79	STOCK UNIT	STOCK £p	USAGE UNIT	USAGE £p
	B			562.92		329.22
	I			180.42		98.44
	M			99.81		10.72
	O			165.20		(37.92)
	A			979.28		1084.57
	N			272.38		207.97
	L			181.45		67.52
	K			55.48		25.13
	J			67.13		13.87
	G			221.00		258.97
	H			35.50		33.85
	F			154.65		98.21
	E			293.49		245.00
	D			164.81		5.75
	C			64.00		53.04
				3868.29		2475.49
	P			1.13		80.24
	P			—		—

GROUP COST DECREASE/INCREASE

WEEK 2

8.10.79 - 14.10.79

	GROUPS	DECREASE	INCREASES	
WET STOCK	MEAT		20.40	
	FISH		12.30	
	POULTRY	4.62		
	FRUIT/VEG		39.49	
	DAIRY	18.65		
	BREAD		2.68	
	TOTAL	23.27	74.87	
	INCREASE		51.60	.44% of total wet stock purchases
DRY STOCK	VARIOUS	18.59	22.75	
	TOTAL	18.59	22.75	
	INCREASE		4.16	.15% of total dry stores issues
	TOTALS	41.86	97.62	
	INCREASES		55.76	.38% of total gross cost

Finalising the food cost report

For the actual food cost report you will need the *goods received record sheets* and the *dry stores requisition sheet* from the bought ledger department. At the botton of these sheets will be total of goods received for each commodity. This information is also collated by the bought ledger department from the invoices relating to goods bought during the week. The totals should be entered under the correct day and commodity group on the food report sheet (see pages 74 and 75). When entering these figures *do not* enter dry goods purchase figures. Dry goods are sent to the store rather than the kitchen. It is requisitions of dry goods to the kitchen which show consumption rather than purchase figures. Liquor figures can be taken from cellar requisitions.

Having gathered these figures the *gross cost* figure can be found by adding the wet stock total to the dry goods and liquor requisitions for each day. As well as adding daily figures across, commodity group figures for the week should be added down the page and then these totals added across to check the gross cost figure.

The staff food allowance figures can be obtained from a staff allowance food cost report (page 77). This should be subtracted from the gross cost figures to give *net cost*.

The *total revenue* figures are obtained from the daily revenue report. The food cost percentage figure is the food cost expressed as a percentage of revenue. This can be calculated by multiplying the net cost by one hundred and dividing by the total revenue.

Total opening stock is the closing stock figure from the previous week's food cost report. If opening stock is added to total food purchase for the week we can find the value of all the food that was already in or has come into the operation during the week. If we substract closing stock value from this we find the consumption of each commodity group during the week. The closing stock value is obtained from the weekly stocktake results.

The overall actual food cost percentage result is now calculated using the net food cost total and the total revenue. The net cost is multiplied by one hundred and divided by total revenue (see pages 74 and 75).

Stores stocktaking

The ultimate control over the stores is achieved by taking physical stock of all dry goods items on a monthly basis. The stocktake should be compared with the stores ledger and should there be any difference, the inventory can be also checked against the bin cards. In order to prepare a reconciliation between physical stock and ledger stock it is necessary to maintain a separate analysis of stores purchases. (See page 76)

COMMODITY ANALYSIS
WET STOCK

	1979	MEAT	FISH	POULTRY	FRUIT/VEG	DAIRY	BREAD	SUB TOTAL WET STOCK
MONDAY	8.10	1733.01	138.74	414.06	233.31	404.73	224.77	3148.62
TUESDAY	9.10	479.85	140.83	72.80	279.84	320.05	224.98	1518.35
WEDNESDAY	10.10	1014.52	168.29	11.55	134.98	253.79	232.80	1815.93
THURSDAY	11.10	318.63	91.23	99.68	338.07	70.89	115.68	1034.18
FRIDAY	12.10	1043.98	381.05	275.16	261.93	992.02	198.63	3152.77
SATURDAY	13.10	112.78	29.70	108.80	160.73	90.72	164.36	667.09
SUNDAY	14.10	-------	------	------	174.52	83.64	146.84	405.00
TOTAL		4702.77	949.84	982.05	1583.38	2215.84	1308.06	11741.94
% OF PURCHASES		32.13%	6.5%	6.71%	10.82%	15.14%	8.94%	80.24%
TOTAL OF OPENING STOCK		3828.95	1053.12	519.98	824.87	1404.69	749.00	8380.61
% OF TOTAL STOCKHOLDING		32.14%	8.84%	4.36%	6.92%	11.79%	6.29%	70.34%
SUB TOTAL		8531.72	2002.96	1502.03	2408.25	3620.53	2057.06	20122.55
TOTAL CLOSING STOCK		3161.19	1015.48	845.05	725.36	1614.07	839.85	8201.00
% OF TOTAL STOCKHOLDING		26.2%	8.41%	7%	6%	13.37%	6.96%	67.94%
TOTAL CONSUMPTION		5370.53	987.48	656.98	1682.89	2006.46	1217.21	11921.55
% OF TOTAL CONSUMPTION		37.1%	6.82%	4.54%	11.62%	13.86%	8.41%	82.35%
MINUS ALLOWANCE								
ACTUAL COST								
THIS WEEK'S COST INCREASE		20.40	12.30	------	39.49	--------	2.68	74.87
COST INCREASE				4.62		18.65		23.27
TOTAL COST INCREASE								51.60
% OF INCREASE/DECR. OF PURCHASES		.43%	1.29%	(.47)	2.49%	(.84%)	.2%	.44%

REMARKS

PREPARED BY CHECKED BY

DRY STOCK STORES	LIQUOR	GROSS COST	STAFF ALLOWANCES	TODAY	TO DATE	TODAY	TO DATE	FOOD COST & TO DATE
730.48	14.66	3893.76	428.00	3465.76	3465.76	4699.39	4699.39	73.7%
176.49	-----	1694.84	427.00	1267.84	4733.60	3816.89	8516.28	55.6%
824.13	11.99	2652.05	427.00	2225.05	6958.65	5468.63	13984.91	49.7%
172.78	-----	1206.96	427.00	779.96	7738.61	4283.58	18268.43	42.4%
711.47	22.41	3886.65	427.00	3459.65	11198.26	6052.14	24320.63	46%
215.37	10.40	892.86	427.00	465.86	11664.12	6695.34	31015.97	37.6%
------	2.60	470.60	427.00	(19.40)	11664.72	3994.03	35010.00	33.3%
2820.72	62.06	14634.72	2990.00	11644.72				
19.34%	.42%							
3513.06	19.31	11912.98						
29.5%	.16%	100%						
6343.78	81.37	26547.70						
3868.29	1.13	12070.42						
32.05%	.01%	100%						
2475.49	80.24	14477.28	2990.00		11487.28			32.8%
17.1%	.55%	100%			287.00			
					11200.28			31.99%
4.16	----	79.03						
		23.27						
		55.76						
.15%		.38%						

STAFF COUNT
520

STOCKHOLDING

11912.98		
12070.42		
157.44	INCREASE	
1.3%	INCREASE	

OTHER ALLOWANCES

OFF SALES	2.00
BAR ALLOWANCES	120.00
MARKETING	165.00
TOTAL	287.00

Monthly stores reconciliation

Opening stock (actual)	£ 9 840.63	Ledger/bincards should be identical
Plus stores purchases	£11 486.81	Information from goods inwards sheet and delivery notes
	£21 327.44	
Less issues	£10 830.72	see monthly requisitions
Closing stock (potential)	£10 496.72	totals from ledger balances
Closing stock (actual)	£10 511.34	as per physical stocktake
Stock variance	+ £ 14.62	

Four-weekly requisition summary

Week one	£ 2 878.60
two	2 830.72
three	2 674.83
four	2 446.57
Total	£10 830.72

Off sales

There are certain occasions when one wishes to sell products at cost or cost plus a handling charge to customers or staff. If this is a regular event it will, most likely, be planned and organised. It is important to control this however often it happens and the procedure is quite simple.

1 Introduce a requisition book for beverage off sales and another for food off sales.
2 All requests for off sales must be authorised by the Food and Beverage Manager or his assistant.
3 Nothing should be issued until an authorised requisition form has been presented.
4 All money should be collected immediately from the purchaser.
5 When money is paid to the cashier ensure that the money is correctly accounted for and that the correct accounts code is shown on any documentation.
6 The cashier's receipt is to be attached to the authorised requisition and this is then left in the requisition book.
7 The original requisition will go with other requisitions from the department to the Food and Beverage Controller, who will marry up the copies.

Any missing dockets or discrepancies between copies should be reported and checked immediately. At the end of each accounting period a list of all off sales transactions with requisition and receipt numbers should be sent to the accounts department. It is important that the money received does not go normally into daily revenue or it will distort potential/actual results.

Staff allowances

Food cost control will only be accurate and complete if one treats the feeding of staff as another outlet. To credit an established cost allowance is not enough. A chef could cover up inefficient production by reducing staff meal costs below the allowance or conversely food costs could be affected by a staff meal allowance which is not large enough. For this reason staff meals must be planned, agreed, costed and regularly re-examined. Recipe cards for staff meals can be utilised and recosted weekly if necessary. A separate report of actual staff meal costs should be produced each week and compared with the allowance.

Weekly staff cost summary Week 2

Monday to Sunday, 8.10.79 – 11.10.79	This week	To date
	£	£
Breakfast	167.44	354.88
Various costs such as: milk, cream, rolls, coffee, tea	481.69	963.38
Salad bar	481.69	436.02
Menu No 1 mince pie	252.70	512.63
Menu No 2 pork chop	301.20	669.47
Menu No 3 turkey	256.88	582.81
Menu No 4 plaice	161.23	472.49
Menu No 5 spaghetti	191.23	506.26
Menu No 6 lamb	303.91	512.44
Menu No 7 chicken	223.45	465.39
Night staff meals	280.00	545.40
Total actual cost	2 832.74	6 021.17
Allowance	2 990.00*	5 980.00
	– 157.26	+ 41.17

* Refer to page 75

Comparison of potential usage and actual usage

It is imperative to do such comparisons regularly for all items whether high or low cost. Some exercises are more complicated than others but all are worthwhile. On page 79 is an exercise on some bread items.

Numbers served: 8.10.79 – 14.10.79		Potential Usage		
		Croissants	**Rolls**	**Toast**
1842	English breakfast	1842	1842	1323 loaves
4247	Continental breakfast	4247	4247	303 loaves
420	Staff breakfast		420	30 loaves
6509	Total (inc of staff)	6089	6509	465 loaves
1818	Lunch		1818	12 loaves
2604	Dinner		2604	47 loaves
4422	Total		4422	59 loaves
	Grand total	6089	10931	524 loaves
			Actual Usage	
		(1)	(2)	(3)
	Total	5028	11375	524 loaves
	–/+ Potential usage	–1061	+ 444	nil

(1) Refer to actual usage, stock sheet line A6 (page 69). 419 dozen = 5028
(2) Refer to A1 to A4 (page 69)
(3) Refer to A7 (page 69)
Numbers served refer to potential food cost sheets – sales analysis for each outlet (pages 82 to 89).

The weekly potential food cost report

The calculation of potential food cost and its comparison with actual food cost is an easy way of analysing the accuracy of food costs in the operation or a particular part of it. It is an excellent method of food cost control. For this exercise you will need:

1 A Sales analysis of each dish. This can be obtained from bills or, if you have a coded cash register system, from an audit roll. Each item should be recorded on a standard worksheet for each department.
2 The worksheet will have the following column titles (see page 86).
 (a) *Items* All items sold in the particular outlet. This should include any items not listed on the menu.
 (b) *Codes* Numbers or letters identifying each dish on an audit roll or menu.
 (c) *Day and date* If appropriate, the day can be divided into separate lunch and dinner columns or other divisions. The actual division should remain constant, however, to allow comparisons over time.
 (d) *Total column* Weekly totals of the sales of each item.
 (e) *Potential cost* for each single item.
 (f) *Total potential cost* of the weekly sales of each item.

(g) *Menu/dish selling price*, excluding VAT for each single item.
(h) *Total potential revenue* for the week's sales of the item excluding VAT.
(i) *Percentage of total sales* accounted for by each item.

3 Standard recipes should be agreed and costed with the chef. Use a recipe cost card and list and cost all ingredients according to current food costs. The costing should include a tolerance for a certain amount of waste and for items that may be to small to cost individually – salt, pepper, and other seasonings, for example. A tolerance of five per cent is not unrealistic for most of these dishes included in this exercise.

RECIPE FOR CONTINENTAL BREAKFAST CODE No. ☐☐☐☐☐

QUANTITY PRODUCED ONE PORTIONS

RESTAURANT

PORTION SIZE ______ – ______

PORTION SIZE ______ – ______

UNIT	INGREDIENTS	DATE		DATE		DATE		DATE	
		AT	AMOUNT	AT	AMOUNT	AT	AMOUNT	AT	AMOUNT
5 fl oz	Orange or Gr Juice	*	.0405						
1	Roll	2.65x100	.0265						
1	Croissant	60p doz.	.05						
2	Butter	13.70(400)	.034						
½	Jam	5.47(100)	.0274						
1	Marmalade	5.14(100)	.0514						
1	Honey	5.15(100)	.0515						
1 sl	Toast	27p (14s)	.02						
1	Tea or coffee	*	.105						
			.4063						
	Plus 5%		.0203						
			42.66						
	TOTAL COST		42.66						
	COST PER PORTION		43						

LT/A42

4 A summary sheet, for all outlets, of potential and actual revenue comparison. In order to establish potential food cost, you should multiply the numbers of each item sold by the recipe cost and enter this into the total potential cost column. (see page 88)

To establish potential sales revenue you should multiply the number of each item sold by the selling price less VAT. This is entered into the total potential revenue column. The potential food costs of all items and their potential revenue can then be added to produce two grand totals. From this can be calculated the potential food cost percentage for an operation based on a particular week's sales mix. This potential food cost percentage can then be compared with the actual food cost percentage for the same period.

If a large number of recipes are involved, it may be very difficult to recost standard recipes immediately after each increase or decrease in the price of commodities. I therefore record on the weekly purchase sheets the change in cost of each item where applicable and take these figures into account when I do the weekly or monthly comparison of actual and potential costs as below.

Week 2 revenue

Potential revenue	£35 010.48
Actual revenue	35 010.00
Under potential	£ 0.48 only

Week 2 food cost

Potential cost	£11 061.67
Actual cost	11 200.28
Over potential	£ 138.61
Minus the weekly cost increases which were not yet adjustged on the recipe cards to find the new potential cost	–55.76
	£ 82.85

or expressed differently:

Week 2 food cost

Potential cost	£11 061.67	
Plus cost increases	55.76	(refer to page 72)
Final potential cost	11 117.43	
Actual cost	11 200.28	
Over potential	£ 82.85	

Week 2 food cost percentage

	Potential	*Actual*
Revenue	£35 010.48	£35 010.00
Cost	11 061 67	11 200.28
	31.59% (31.6%)	31.99% (32%)
Plus increase	£ 55.76	
Final potential revenue	£11 117.34	
Final potential cost	31.75%	

Potential food cost worksheet. Period 8th October to 14th October. Outlet "one".

Code	Items	Mon 8	Tues 9	Wed 10	Thur 11	Fri 12	Sat 13	Sun 14	Total	Potential cost per menu	Total potential cost	Menu price excluding VAT	Total potential revenue	% sales
O 1		3	2	2	3	3	2	3	18	.37	6.66			
O 2		6	6	11	5	6	10	2	46	.99	45.54			
O 3		15	18	17	16	19	18	18	121	.51	61.71			
O 4		2	2	5	5	—	—	2	16	1.10	17.60			
O 5		3	4	3	6	4	6	4	30	.58	17.40			
O 6		1	2	3	7	5	3	—	22	.94	20.68			
O 7		4	2	1	6	3	4	3	23	.57	13.11			
O 8		—	1	4	—	—	2	—	7	.67	4.69			
O 9		—	1	2	1	—	—	—	4	.36	1.44			
O10		2	2	1	3	2	1	—	11	.33	3.63			
O11		1	2	2	1	8	1	—	19	.36	6.84			
O12		3	2	5	1	1	1	1	14	.40	5.60			
O13		2	—	—	1	—	—	—	3	.33	.99			
O14		2	9	5	2	2	3	4	27	.38	10.26			
O15		—	—	—	2	4	—	2	8	.54	4.32			
O16		1	5	1	—	—	3	2	12	.75	9.00			
O17		4	4	5	1	6	6	2	28	.97	27.16			
O18		7	3	1	5	5	7	5	33	.64	21.12			
O19		8	6	5	4	3	7	4	32	2.59	82.88			
O20		3	3	3	3	—	2	1	14	1.66	23.24			
O21		6	15	11	10	7	11	10	70	2.21	154.70			
O22		2	4	6	4	7	9	7	39	1.29	50.31			
O23		7	11	23	17	16	11	7	92	1.64	150.88			
O24		7	2	1	4	5	3	—	22	1.15	25.30			
O25		35	39	45	48	51	50	34	302	.19	57.38			
O26		31	37	40	49	47	47	30	281	.26	73.06			
O27		2	6	1	1	2	1	—	13	.19	2.47			
O28		4	2	2	—	4	3	—	15	.20	3.00			
O29		2	—	—	1	—	1	1	5	.17	.85			
O30		—	—	—	1	—	—	2	8	.25	2.00			
O31		4	3	11	—	10	7	7	42	.34	14.28			
O32		46	38	58	64	51	43	48	348	.24	83.52			
O33		14	16	18	13	14	20	21	116	.30	34.80			
O34		43	44	69	56	48	50	33	348	.04	13.92			
O35		[illegible]	[illegible]	[illegible]	[illegible]	[illegible]	[illegible]	[illegible]	[illegible]	[illegible]	[illegible]			

P 2	5	2	3	6	11	5	5	37	.30	11.10			
P 3	1	—	—	2	3	—	—	6	.36	2.16			
P 4	7	4	3	5	10	2	7	38	1.64	62.32			
P 5	5	5	—	11	12	5	2	40	.97	38.80			
P 6	12	9	3	16	19	5	5	69	.26	17.94			
P 7	12	8	3	16	19	5	5	68	.19	12.92			
S 1	3	—	1	1	2	—	—	7	.37	2.59			
S 2	5	6	—	13	—	2	—	26	.51	13.26			
S 3	4	7	—	1	2	—	—	14	.33	4.62			
S 4	8	4	—	9	—	—	—	21	1.64	34.44			
S 5	1	1	1	2	2	—	—	5	.75	3.75			
S 6	4	2	1	6	—	1	—	14	.97	13.58			
S 7	13	6	1	14	4	1	—	39	.26	10.14			
S 8	13	6	1	14	4	1	—	39	.19	7.41			
S 9 Various costs										44.64			
										1386.15			
Supplement charges	12	8	10	6	4	10	10	60			1.20½	72.30	2.1
Set menu "O"	44	53	53	50	55	48	36	339		(1088.63)	7.95	2695.05	78.6
Set menu "P"	13	7	3	13	4	3	1	44		(163.10)	6.04	265.76	7.7
Set menu "S"	12	11	3	16	20	7	9	78		(134.43)	5.09	397.02	11.6
Covers	69	71	59	79	79	58	46	461		1386.15		3430.13	10.0%

Outlet one had originally only one set priced menu (here menu O) with a supplement charge for various items. This menu was mainly sold between 20.00 and 23.00 hrs. In order to attract business a pre-theatre menu was introduced between 18.00 and 19.00 hrs (set menu P) at a very reduced price and a supper menu (menu S) from 23.00 hrs to closing time. It was therefore essential to watch very carefully these three menus if one wanted to stay within the average overall food cost of this outlet.

	Cost	Potential rev	Ratio %	Cost %
Menu O	1088.63	2767.35	80.68	39.34
Menu P	163.10	265.76	7.75	61.37
Menu S	134.43	397.02	11.57	33.86
Total	1386.16	3430.13	100	40.41

Potential food cost worksheet. Period 8th October to 14th October. Outlet "two".

Items	Code	Mon 8	Tues 9	Wed 10	Thurs 11	Fri 12	Sat 13	Sun 14	Total	Potential cost per menu	Total potential cost	Menu excluding VAT	Total potential revenue	% sales
	ME ET	18	9	17	4	8	5	12	282	.09	25.38	.45	126.90	6.84
	ME CB	33	30	58	34	37	39	41	272	.45	122.40	1.40	380.80	19.94
	ME 4	30	11	14	12	17	16	23	123	.18	22.14	.80	98.40	5.15
	ME 3	23	18	13	11	18	21	16	120	.30	36.00	.80	96.00	5.03
	ME 2	11	7	12	12	5	7	11	65	.18	11.70	.80	52.00	2.7
	ME 1	13	14	11	3	14	14	15	84	.33	27.72	.90	75.60	3.9
	ME 5	1	1	2	2	1	1	—	8	.29	2.32	.80	6.40	.3
	ME 49	7	8	7	6	5	5	7	45	.15	6.75	.60	27.00	1.4
	ME 50	3	2	4	3	—	5	1	18	.20	3.60	.60	10.80	.6
	ME 8	—	1	1	—	1	1	—	4	.70	2.80	2.40	9.60	.5
	ME 9	3	6	5	4	3	7	5	33	.78	25.74	2.40	79.20	4.1
	ME 20	3	7	4	2	—	1	1	18	.19	3.42	.50	9.00	.5
	ME 21	3	—	3	—	—	4	2	12	.28	3.36	.80	9.60	.5
	ME 30	5	1	1	—	—	3	4	14	.23	3.22	.90	9.80	.5
	ME 12	8	8	7	4	2	6	4	39	.79	30.81	2.70	105.30	5.5
	ME 6	9	10	8	4	5	1	4	41	.51	20.91	2.75	112.75	5.9
	ME 9	10	3	5	4	—	6	3	31	1.05	32.55	3.50	108.50	5.7
	ME 5	2	2	4	1	4	5	3	21	.85	17.85	3.20	67.20	3.5
	ME 51	4	2	—	—	—	1	—	7	.10	0.70	.30	2.10	.1
	ME 72	—	—	1	—	—	—	1	2	.10	0.20	.30	0.60	.03
	ME 66	9	5	5	1	4	2	5	31	.21	6.51	.65	20.15	1.05
	ME 68	2	7	1	1	3	4	—	18	.12	2.16	.50	9.00	.5
	ME 70	1	3	1	1	—	1	—	7	.17	1.19	.70	4.90	.26
	ME 69	3	3	2	2	—	1	2	13	.24	3.12	.70	9.10	.5
	ME 67	—	1	1	—	—	—	3	5	.20	1.00	.80	4.00	.21
	ME102	7	15	22	10	18	14	18	104	.05	5.20	.30	31.20	1.6
	ME 33	1	3	6	4	6	6	5	31	.04	1.24	.20	6.20	.3

Potential food cost worksheet. Period 8th October to 14th October. Outlet "two". (continued)

Items	Code	Mon 8	Tues 9	Wed 10	Thurs 11	Fri 12	Sat 13	Sun 14	Total	Potential cost per menu	Total potential cost	Menu excluding VAT	Total potential revenue	% sales
	ME 48	2	2	5	1	1	1	2	14	.03	0.42	0.10	1.40	.07
	ME 39	53	47	63	49	80	80	67	439	.08	35.12	.35	153.65	8.04
	ME 34	37	67	45	49	55	60	38	351	.10	36.85	.35	122.85	6.43
	ME 56	13	15	15	18	13	19	15	108	.07	7.56	.25	27.00	1.4
	ME 36	6	2	2	5	6	3	8	32	.08	2.56	.35	11.20	.59
	ME 38	12	5	2	3	—	1	—	23	.08	1.84	.35	8.05	.42
	ME 35	—	—	—	—	—	4	3	7	.08	0.56	.35	2.45	.13
	ME 52	4	1	—	1	1	2	1	10	.31	3.10	.95	9.50	.5
	ME 61	—	—	2	—	—	2	3	7	.28	1.96	.95	6.65	.35
	ME 53	—	—	—	—	—	—	10	10	.29	2.90	1.10	11.00	.56
	ME100	20	21	27	30	23	28	28	177	.05	8.85	.25	44.25	2.32
	ME 41	4		1	—	—	3	1	9	.07	0.63	.25	2.25	.12
	ME101	12	17	4	8	12	27	14	94	.06	5.64	.25	23.50	1.23
	ME103		4						4	1.11	4.44	3.50	14.00	.73
											532.42		1909.85	100%

Potential food cost worksheet   Period 8th October to 14th October   Outlet three

Code	Item	Mon 8	Tues 9	Wed 10	Thur 11	Fri 12	Sat 13	Sun 14	Total	Potential cost per menu	Total potential cost	Menu price excluding VAT	Total potential revenue	% sales
FL	Continental BR	223	226	307	285	305	237	259	1842	44.693	823.24	1.40	2578.80	100%

Potential food cost worksheet   Period 8th October to 14th October   Outlet four

Menu number/type	Mon 8	Tues 9	Wed 10	Thur 11	Fri 12	Sat 13	Sun 14	Total	Potential cost per menu	Total potential cost	Menu price excluding VAT	Total potential revenue	% sales
31			135					135	2.26	305.10	800	1080.00	14.45
36					158			158	1.75	276.50	5.48	865.84	11.58
37	140							140	1.97	275.86	6.05	847.00	11.33
42						70		70	2.72	190.40	8.50	595.00	7.96
	84							84	0.80	67.20	2.60	218.40	2.92
Coffee & biscuits			7	7	185			199	0.11	21.89	0.45	89.55	1.2
Sandwiches					10			10	0.23	2.30	0.65	6.50	0.09
Special menu at £6.05			39	39	185			263	1.96	515.48	6.05	1591.15	21.28
menu at £5.65						350		350	1.83	640.50	5.65	1977.50	26.45
menu at £2.35					70			70	2.35*	164.50	2.35	164.50*	2.2
canapes		39								12.80		40.00	0.54
										2472.47		7475.44	100%

Potential food cost worksheet. Period from 8th October to 14th October. Outlet "five".

Items	Code	Mon 8	Tues 9	Wed 10	Thur 11	Fri 12	Sat 13	Sun 14	Total	Potential cost per menu	Total potential cost	Menu price excluding VAT	Total potential revenue	% sales
	FRAN	1	1	4	5	9	7	—	27	.37	9.99	1.48	39.96	2.06%
	FISH	4	6	10	19	33	20	12	115	.23	26.45	1.48	170.20	8.78%
	BOWL		2	2	7	4	2		17	.16	2.72	0.83	14.11	0.73%
	KING	1		3	5	5	2		16	1.15	18.40	2.91	46.56	2.4%
	SALD				1	2	1		4	.32	1.28	1.65	6.60	.34%
	OCEN	2	4	3	1	5	5	5	25	.36	9.00	1.78	44.50	2.3%
	GUAC		2	2	6	4	3	1	18	.38	6.89	1.78	32.04	1.65%
	FOXY	4	5	4	7	20	3	3	46	.92	43.32	3.70	170.20	8.78%
	MEX	17	17	19	18	44	28	14	157	.39	61.23	2.35	368.95	19.04%
	PIZA	8	4	9	12	28	10	11	82	.39	31.98	1.48	121.36	6.26%
	SAM	1	8	4	15	9	11	2	51	1.20	61.20	3.65	186.15	9.6%
	PORK		2	1	3	4	2	2	14	1.20	16.80	3.61	80.54	2.61%
	DELI	5		4	3	5	5	2	24	.75	18.00	2.65	63.60	3.28%
	CHAR	1	2	2	5	8	—	1	19	.93	17.67	2.74	52.06	2.69%
	TURK	4	4	4	7	11	5	3	34	.47	15.98	2.65	90.10	4.65%
	SIDE	2	2	2	2	9	1		18	.17	3.06	0.65	11.70	.6%
	LARG						1		1	.43	0.43	1.96	1.96	.1%
	WALD	5			3	5	3		16	.33	5.28	1.13	18.08	.93%
	YANK	2	1		4	1	3		11	.22	2.42	0.96	10.56	.54%
	BIG	4	8	12	6	11	8	4	53	.39	20.67	1.65	87.45	4.51%
	SCOP	1	1	1	5	3	1	1	13	.27	3.51	0.96	12.48	.64%
	FARM		1	2	1	3	2		9	.29	2.61	1.22	10.98	.57%
	HAWI	1	4		3	2		2	12	.25	3.00	1.22	14.64	.75%
	FLIR	1			1	1	3	1	6	.18	1.08	1.22	7.32	.38%
	ALSK			3	2	5	2		12	.32	3.84	1.22	14.64	.76%
	APLE		2	5	2	6		4	19	.21	3.99	1.22	23.18	1.2%
	CHES	2	2		6	8	1	6	25	.30	7.50	1.13	28.25	1.46%
	LNCH	4							4	1.47	5.88	5.22	20.88	1.08%
	LNCH									1.19	—	4.30		
	COFF	37	14	24	35	40	51	25	226	.20	45.20	0.70	158.20	8.17%
	TEA	10	4	6	4	6	11	9	50	.14	7.00	0.52	26.00	1.34%
	MISC										21.69		34.81	1.8%
	Total										478.02		1938.06	100%

Potential food cost worksheet. Period 8th October to 14th October. Outlet "six".

Code	Items	Mon 8	Tues 9	Wed 10	Thur 11	Fri 12	Sat 13	Sun 14	Total	Potential cost per menu	Total potential cost	Menu price excluding VAT	Total potential revenue	% sales
CB		342	272	273	328	335	282	301	2133	0.43	917.19	1.40	2986.20	16.89
EB		393	292	262	204	189	206	212	1758	0.82	1441.56	2.66	4570.80	25.86
1		19	16	24	28	17	6	14	124	0.49	60.70	1.60	198.40	1.12
2		9	8	10	8	6	9	8	58	0.44	25.52	1.45	84.10	0.48
3		5	7	9	6	3	5	4	39	0.32	12.48	1.10	42.90	0.24
4		3	4	1	7	4	4	4	27	0.51	13.77	1.70	45.90	0.26
5		2	2	7	4	—	—	—	15	0.56	8.40	1.85	27.75	0.16
6		6	—	3	7	9	5	9	39	0.32	12.48	1.40	54.60	0.31
7		14	16	28	22	22	18	15	135	0.35	47.25	1.10	148.80	0.84
8		38	26	24	34	38	35	49	244	0.22	53.68	0.75	183.00	1.04
9		40	34	20	34	28	51	29	236	0.28	66.08	1.00	236.00	1.34
10		31	22	26	23	17	35	31	185	0.26	48.10	1.60	296.00	1.68
11		28	19	17	25	16	29	31	163	0.42	68.08	1.90	309.70	1.75
12		6	5	7	5	7	10	22	62	0.55	34.10	2.20	136.40	0.8
13		35	26	30	28	22	23	7	171	0.81	138.51	2.70	461.70	2.61
14		18	9	9	15	18	14	18	101	0.87	87.87	2.80	282.80	1.6
15		20	22	13	34	21	15	32	147	1.62	238.14	4.90	720.30	4.07
16		13	11	13	25	7	8	6	83	1.71	141.93	5.00	415.00	2.35
17		15	7	13	14	10	7	4	70	1.08	75.60	4.20	294.00	1.70
18		18	11	14	24	19	14	18	119	1.26	149.94	3.95	470.00	2.70
19		31	6	20	14	20	27	22	140	0.76	106.40	2.70	378.00	2.14
20		8	11	10	4	8	9	11	60	1.20	61.20	3.30	198.00	1.12
21		34	16	16	24	17	18	30	155	0.97	150.35	3.20	496.00	2.81
22		10	4	9	1	7	3	9	43	0.73	31.39	2.90	124.70	0.71
23		16	11	20	15	22	11	18	113	0.90	101.70	2.90	327.70	1.85
24		10	5	18	22	12	13	13	93	0.85	79.05	2.80	260.40	1.5
25		7	11	5	5	7	9	10	54	0.67	36.18	2.70	145.80	0.82
26		2	2	3	—	—	—	3	10	0.73	7.30	2.90	29.00	0.16
27		8	—	4	2	1	1	2	14	1.40	19.60	3.90	54.60	0.31
28		2	2	6	1	3	3	3	20	0.85	17.00	2.90	58.00	0.33
29		14	20	11	15	19	31	11	121	0.69	83.49	2.20	266.20	1.51

Potential food cost worksheet. Period 8th October to 14th October. Outlet "six".

Code	Items	Mon 8	Tues 9	Wed 10	Thur 11	Fri 12	Sat 13	Sun 14	Total	Potential cost per menu	Total potential cost	Menu price excluding VAT	Total potential revenue	% sales
30		3	4	2	3	4	6	1	23	0.47	10.81	1.60	36.80	0.21
31		1	9	10	12	9	15	9	65	0.75	48.75	2.20	143.00	0.81
32		9	18	2	6	8	12	13	68	0.79	53.78	2.70	183.60	1.04
33		4	4	6	1	7	9	4	35	0.43	15.05	1.45	50.75	0.3
34		22	17	18	17	10	14	8	106	0.18	19.08	0.90	95.40	0.54
35		19	8	14	8	9	13	19	90	0.19	17.60	0.60	54.00	0.31
36		32	27	25	30	32	37	40	223	0.16	35.68	0.70	156.10	0.9
36		33	28	25	31	31	37	40	225	0.22	49.50	0.70	157.50	0.9
37										0.04		0.50		
38		—	1	2	—	—	—	—	3	0.23	0.69	0.80	2.40	0.01
39		22	32	22	23	17	14	20	150	0.30	45.00	1.05	157.80	0.9
40		7	6	5	12	5	8	11	54	0.15	8.10	0.55	29.70	0.2
41		4	10	10	11	10	12	5	62	0.28	17.36	0.80	49.60	0.3
42		100	85	82	102	95	124	139	727	0.06	43.62	0.35	254.45	1.44
43		277	193	192	281	261	228	259	1430	0.11	157.30	0.35	500.50	2.83
		30	8	6	18	24	15	37	138	0.29	40.02	0.80	110.40	0.62
	Tour menus													
	140 £4.70								140	1.50	210.00	4.70	658.00	4.2
	36 £2.34								36	0.75	27.00	2.34	84.24	
	Miscellaneous revenue	(118.10	378.38	412.60	202.78	41.25	65.17	132.82	1351.60)		234.34		608.86	3.44
											5369.37		17678.20	100%

Food outlets Period 8.10 to 14.10.79

	One		Two		Three		Four		Five		Six		Total	
	Potential	Actual	Potential	Actual	Potential	Actual	Potential	Actual	Potential	Actual	Potential	Actual	Potential	Actual
Revenue	3430.13	3405.41	1909.85	1914.29	2578.80	2578.80	7475.44	7475.44	1938.06	1947.80	17678.80	17688.20	35010.48	35010.00
Cost	1386.15		532.42		823.24		2472.47		478.02		5369.37		11061.67	11200.28
Cost %	40.41%		27.88%		31.92%		33.07%		24.66%		30.37%		31.59%	31.99%
% of sale		9.7%		5.5%		7.4%		21.3%		5.6%		50.5%		100%

In this particular week the summary does not show very much which needs to be explained, with the exception of outlet one, where the cost is very high.

If you refer to the potential food cost sheet (page 83) of outlet one you will see that the high cost was caused by menu P, a pre-theatre menu at a cost of 61.37%, which was successfully introduced for the very early evening.

Four-weekly revenue 1.10.79–28.10.79

	Potential	Actual	Difference	
Week 1	37290.24	37324.42	34.18	over
2	35010.48	35010.00	0.48	under
3	32619.02	32728.53	109.51	over
4	35693.13	35683.90	9.23	under
Period	140612.87	140746.85	133.98	over potential

Four-weekly cost

	Potential	Actual	Difference		Weekly cost increases
Week 1	11426.52	11765.37	338.85	over	38.29
2	11061.67	11200.28	138.61	over	55.76
3	10135.68	10071.26	64.46	under	11.48
4	10698.09	10850.41	152.32	over	41.40
Period	43321.96	43887.32	565.32	over potential	146.93

Four-weekly cost %

Week 1	30.6 %	31.5%
2	31.6 %	32.0%
3	31.1 %	30.8%
4	30 %	30.4%
Period	30.81%	31.2%

	43321.96	
Cost Increase	146.93	
Adjusted Potential Cost	43468.89	
	30.19%	31.2%

Price increase analysis record outlet "six". Period one year.

Items	Code	% of sales	% increase	New % of sales based on original revenue
	CB	16.89	25.64	21.22
	EB	25.86	16.02	30.00
	1	1.12	10.4	1.24
	2	0.48	—	0.48
	3	0.24	16.6	0.28
	4	0.26	17.9	0.31
	5	0.16	20.4	0.19
	6	0.31	15.9	0.36
	7	0.84	—	0.84
	8	1.04	20.3	1.25
	9	1.34	26.6	1.7
	10	1.68	15.4	1.94
	11	1.75	23.8	2.17
	12	0.8	10.0	0.88
	13	2.61	—	2.61
	14	1.6	19.4	1.91
	15	4.07	28.3	5.22
	16	2.35	23.6	2.90
	17	1.70	23.1	2.09
	18	2.70	19.3	3.22
	19	2.14	26.2	2.70
	20	1.12	17.4	1.31
	21	2.81	25.0	3.51
	22	0.71	16.08	0.82
	23	1.85	11.28	2.06
	24	1.5	20.6	1.81
	25	0.82	4.2	0.85
	26	0.16	14.9	0.18
	27	0.31	4.7	0.32
	28	0.33	4.9	0.35
	29	1.51	11.2	1.68
	30	0.21	10.4	0.23
	31	0.81	16.9	0.95
	32	1.04	14.7	1.19
	33	0.3	3.8	0.31
	34	0.54	11.9	0.60
	35	0.31	7.14	0.33
	36	0.9	—	0.90
	37	0.9	—	0.90
	38	0.01	—	0.01
	39	0.9	—	0.90
	40	0.2	—	0.20
	41	0.3	—	0.30
	42	1.44	—	1.44
	43	2.83	—	2.83
	44	0.62	3.7	0.64
	45	4.2	—	4.2
	46	3.44	14.56	3.94
		100%		116.27%

Price increase analysis record. All outlets of one year's period

	% of sales	% Increase	new % of sale based on Original Revenue
One	9.7%	11.4	10.8
Two	5.5%	10.3	6.07
Three	7.4%	12.1	8.29
Four	21.3%	10.9	23.62
Five	5.6%	14.8	6.43
Six	50.5%	16.27	58.72
	100%		113.93

An overall increase of 13.93%.

Summary of food cost – October 1979. As per controller's four-weekly report

Week	Revenue	Wet stock	Dry stock	Liquor	Staff allowance	Total
One	37 324.42	11431.34	2580.25	83.20	(2749.00)	11345.79
Two	35 010.00	11741.94	2830.72	62.06	(2990.00)	11644.72
Three	32 728.53	11987.16	2521.35	90.44	(2956.00)	11642.95
Four	35 683.90	12373.50	2898.40	140.36	(2956.00)	12456.26
4 weeks	140 746.85	47533.94	10830.72	376.06	(11651.00)	47089.72
	Opening stock week one	9003.64	3606.41	5.16	—	12615.21
	Closing stock week four	(11560.87)	(4240.27)	(16.47)	—	(15817.61)
	Consumption	44976.71	10196.86	364.75	(11651.00)	43887.32

Accounts reconciliation of food cost

Each month the controller's food report should agree with the accounts department's figures. This, of course, does not always happen. If we compare the revenue from the controller's report for October (see page 93) with the revenue from the income journal, we will find a difference of £165.40 which was due to a party served at cost on 12 October in outlet four. (Refer to the worksheet for outlet four on page 86).

Revenue from income journal	140 582.35	Revenue without party at cost
Actual revenue from controller's	140 746.85	Actual revenue over four week period as per Controller's report (page 93).
	164.50	Party at Cost 12.10.79 (refer to worksheet for outlet four)

The total value of wet stock goods received from the controller's report is £47 533.94. The accounts department's total is higher by £1.92. According to the accounts department's nominal ledger the wet stock and dry stock totals were:

Wet stock	£47 613.84
Dry stock	£11 376.41

After further investigation it was found that £79.90 of dry stock was accounted for as wet stock. Even if we combine wet and dry stock figures, however, there is still a difference of £30.50 to be accounted for.

			Wet Stock	**Dry Stock**
Value of wet stock goods received sheet as per accounting	47 535.86	Bought ledger main input	44 760.58	10 438.40
		Main C/B payments	3 395.64	–
		Bought ledger acc.	2 930.13	986.37
		Less C/B receipts	(189.47)	(48.36)
		Less B/L reversal accrual	(3 283.04)	–
			47 613.84	11 376.41
			– 79.90	+ 79.90
Value of wet stock goods from food cost report	47 533.94	Refer to controller's report	47 533.94	11 456.31
Difference	1.92			

Wet stock and dry stock combined

From goods received sheets			From nominal ledger
Wet stock purchases	47 533.94		47 613.84
Dry stock purchases	11 486.81	(see monthly stores requisitions on page 76)	11 376.41
	59 020.75		58 990.25
Difference			30.50
	59 020.75		59 020.75

Food and Beverage items not selling

There are many possible reasons why certain stock is not moving. Two of the most common are that the product is not advertised or that it is forgotten in a corner of the store, cellar or kitchen. It does not take too long to make a note of these items each month and to circularise the relevant departments with your instructions. A pre-typed sheet can be devised as below.

Items Not Moving

Item	Four-week movement	Stock	Instructions for ultilisation
Lychees	nil	32	Use up as soon as possible; do not reorder
Snails and shells	nil	34	" " " " "
Cynar	nil	26	Issue 2 bottles to each bar
Dubonnet Dry	nil	11	" " " " "
Fernet Branca	1	13	Do not reorder until down to 2 bottles
Ginger Wine	1	3	
Martini Rose	nil	17	Issue 2 bottles to each bar
Ricard	nil	11	Issue 2 bottles. Do not reorder
St Raphael	1	nil	Do not reorder
Taylors Port ('71)	nil	10	Issue bottles to each bar. Do not reorder
Schlichte	nil	4	Issue to Bar One. Put on ice and display

9 The cost of a control system

Many operations in the hotel and catering industry neglect control because it is felt that a system would be too costly, that too much work would be involved or that the operation is too large or small to implement an effective control system. At the same time, most managers would acknowledge that money can be lost through lack of control. I would argue that a loss of from three to five per cent is likely if the operation does not know its potentials. In my experience, loss figures are likely to be around five per cent in food production and three per cent in bar outlets. Below are figures for the cost of my own control system.

	One beverage controller	Two food controllers
Desk/table	163	163
Chairs	60	60
Filing cabinet (shared)	43	43
Files	21	21
In/out tray stand	5	5
Bin (shared)	7	7
Ring files	6	6
Calculators	125	125
Shelves (shared)	25	25
Stocktake sheets	–	395
Scales	160 £615	–
Other various utensils	25 pa	40 pa
Photocopies	432 pa	60 pa
Wages (inc of costs) 1 person	4 243.20	2 persons 10 608.00
Totals	5 007.70	11 330.50

The first eleven items can be written off over two years. The total cost per year is £5 007.70 for one beverage controller and £11 330.50 for two food controllers. The total beverage revenue per year is approximately £456 000. From this we can see that, in this case, the break even point is at a revenue of £166 923 if we assume that losses are three per cent per year.

Beverage revenue	**3% of revenue**	**+/− proft/loss**
100 000	3 000.00	−1243.20
141 440	4 243.20	wages break even point
166 923	5 007.70	break even point of total cost for the first two years
456 000	13 680.00	+8672.30 or
		+9436.80 wages only
		− 615.00 equipment/utensils
		− 457.00 photocopies/ utensils
		+8346.80

If we consider that the Controller can be used for both food and beverage control work as necessary it would be worth employing a controller in a smaller outlet with a beverage revenue of about £50 000 and a food revenue of about £150 000. The controller can of course do other clerical work. You will also know your potential revenue without guessing or using rules of thumb. This is important whatever the size of revenue.

In fact, there are considerable savings to be made above the breakeven point.

		+/− Profit/Loss	
Food and beverage revenue	3% of revenue	Less wages and costs after two years	Less wages and costs in first two years
141 433	4 243	breakeven point	− 764
160 000	4 800	+ 557	− 207
166 923	5 007	+ 764	breakeven point
180 000	5 400	+1 157	+ 393
200 000	6 000	+1 757	+ 993
220 000	6 600	+2 357	+1 593

In my particular case, the total revenue per year, for all food outlets is approximately £1 700 000. From the following table you can see that breakeven point is £226 610 if we assume losses of five per cent.

Revenue	5% of revenue	+/− Profit/loss
200 000.00	10 000.00	− 1330.50
226 610.00	11 330.50	breakeven point
300 000.00	15 000.00	+ 3669.50
1 700 000.00	85 000.00	+73 669.50

10 Case study: assessing a new unit by means of two consecutive weeks' control results

A year ago I was asked by my company to introduce the food and beverage control system to an establishment they wished to purchase. It was decided that I should go in on Monday, 16 October to take stock and to get as much information as possible in order to establish potentials in the food and beverage outlets. I went with two of my assistants and my food controller. A very thorough stocktake was done by one of my assistants and myself of each individual unit in the establishment. During the stocktake we recorded any problems or anomalies. The other assistant collected all relevant information on the food and beverage outlets, such as:

the wine list
bar tariffs
menus
the cost of all products bought
duplicates of recent invoices
list of staff and their duties
staff rotas
supplier's names and addresses
the opening and closing times of each outlet
copies of licences

The stocktake was completed in the morning in five and a half hours and after lunch we talked to the owner to complete the following checklist. This I devised some years ago and have always found it to be a great help. There are always occasions when one is confronted by a problem and one wants to know quickly what has gone wrong and how the problem can be rectified. It is then very handy to have such a pre-printed checklist to isolate problems and loopholes in the control system and procedures. The list can be extended or reduced depending on the size and nature of the establishment. It can be particularly useful when taking over the running of a new unit when you wish to pinpoint problems quickly. It can also form the basis of a report and recommendation.

CHECKLIST

AREA/PROCEDURES	COMMENTS FOOD DEPT	RECOMMENDATIONS	COMMENTS BEVERAGE DEPT	RECOMMENDATIONS
A. Purchasing				
1. Who does buying?	Head Chef		No one particularly, mainly Banqueting Manager	With immediate effect Bar Manager should be made responsible for buying
2. Who are the suppliers?	Various	List to be typed out	Various	List to be typed out
3. Who is the buyer responsible to?	Owner		Not applicable	
4. How are the orders placed?				
a) by phone?	Mainly by phone		Mainly by phone	Order form to be completed each time and signed by the Bar Manager
b) in writing?	n/a	Order form to be completed each time and signed by the Head Chef	n/a	
c) representative calls in?	Sometimes		Sometimes	
5. Who's authorising orders?	Nobody	Only Head Chef	Nobody	Only Bar Manager
6. Are there cash purchases?	Yes		Yes	
a) Who checks these items in?	Head Chef		Banqueting Manager	Must be checked in and recorded by Bar Manager
b) Are they itemised?	No	Items must be itemised	No	
7. Are there any copies of specifications?	No	To be introduced later	No	To be introduced later
8. Are orders priced?	No	To be introduced	No	To be introduced

AREA/PROCEDURES	COMMENTS FOOD DEPT	RECOMMENDATIONS	COMMENTS BEVERAGE DEPT	RECOMMENDATIONS
9. Are there price comparisons made with prices from previous purchases?	No		No	
10. Are prenumbered purchase orders used and in sequence?	No	Issued by us	No	Issued by us
A. <u>Purchasing</u>				
11. Are invoices/delivery notes verified?	No	Head Chef	No	Bar Manager
12. Who is authorised to sign invoices?	Accountant		Accountant	
13. Who passes invoices for payment?	Accountant	Method to be continued until further notice	Accountant	Method to be continued until further notice
14. How are invoices dealt with if incorrect?	Accountant		Accountant	
B. <u>Receiving</u>				
1. Who receives the goods?	Head Chef or Sous Chef		Various persons whoever is available	Bar Manager should receive all goods
2. Who locks them away?	Head Chef or Sous Chef		whoever is available	Only Bar Manager should lock things away
3. Are they checked against purchase orders?	Not available	To be introduced	Not available	To be introduced

AREA/PROCEDURES	COMMENTS FOOD DEPT	RECOMMENDATIONS	COMMENTS BEVERAGE DEPT	RECOMMENDATIONS
4. Are containers/empties checked in/out?	n/a		No	To be introduced
5. Are quantities checked?	Yes		Yes	
6. Are cases opened?	Yes		No	
7. Are cases checked for breakages?	Yes		No	
8. Are there established times of delivery?	No	Head Chef arrange with suppliers	No	To be arranged with suppliers
C. <u>Recording of goods</u>				
1. Who does the recording and where?	Accountant		Accountant	Only Bar Manager
2. Who signs the delivery note?	Head Chef		Various people	
3. Is there a daily goods inward record?	Yes		Yes	
4. Are there any standing orders?	No		No	Issue forms from us with explanation
5. How are part deliveries handled?	Not recorded		Not recorded	
6. Is there an error correction list?	No	Issue forms from us with explanation	No	
7. Is there a returned goods list?	No		No	
8. Are all recordings satisfactory?	No		No	

AREA/PROCEDURES	COMMENTS FOOD DEPT	RECOMMENDATIONS	COMMENTS BEVERAGE DEPT	RECOMMENDATIONS
D. Stores				
1. How are the storage facilities?	Not very good	Needed: walk-in fridge	Not very good	More shelves necessary
2. Is the store secure?	Yes		No	Locks to be issued immediately and windows to be repaired
3. Who keeps the keys?	Banqueting Manager/Duty Manager	Duty Manager only	Banqueting Manager/ Duty Manager	Only Bar Manager
4. Who has the authority in case of emergency?	Not established	Re-discuss	Not established	Re-discuss
5. Are the bincards maintained?	No	Already introduced during stocktake	No	Already introduced during stocktake
6. Is the rotation of stock observed?	Not possible to prove yet		Not possible to prove yet	
E. Issuing				
1. Are there specific times?	No	To be introduced	No	To be introduced
2. Who issues stock?	Head Chef self	No need to change	Various persons	Only Bar Manager
3. Are the requisition forms in triplicate?	No	Introduced already by us	No	Introduced already by us
4. Are they accounted for?	No	To be handled by Accountant	Hopefully yes	To be handled by Accountant
5. Are the requisitions priced?	No	To be done by Accountant	No	To be done by Accountant
6. Are the requisitions checked for accuracy?	No	To be checked by Accountant	No	To be checked by Beverage Controller

AREA/PROCEDURES	COMMENTS FOOD DEPT	RECOMMENDATIONS	COMMENTS BEVERAGE DEPT	RECOMMENDATIONS
F. Stocktake				
1. How often is stocktake?	Every three months	Weekly stocktake	Every three months	Weekly stocktake
2. Which areas are they?	2 kitchens, 1 store		3 Bar units/cellar	
3. Who takes the stock?	Head Chef alone	Duty Manager with Head Chef	Banqueting Manager	Beverage Controller
4. Are empties/containers accounted for?	No	Stock already taken	No	Stock already taken
5. Can the inventory be checked via the bin-cards?	No	It is possible from now	No	It is possible from now
6. Where is the stocktake record kept?	With the Accountant	With the Accountant	With the Accountant	With the Accountant
7. Is there a monthly review of slow moving items?	No	Observe weekly	No	Observe weekly
G. Cost %				
1. What is the latest cost?	52%	Cost should be about 40%	62%	Cost should be about 40%
2. Over what period?	11 months	Weekly at least over a month	11 months	Weekly at least over a month
3. What is the budgeted cost?	Not available	Budget figures will be present in two weeks time	Not available	Budget figures will be presented in two weeks time
4. Are the cost % increased over a certain period recorded?	No	Weekly record will give you the cost % increase	No	Weekly record will give you this cost % increase
H. Selling				
1. Who established the prices?	Nobody responsible but Banqueting Manager did certain pricing	A Manager should be responsible Responsibility and system to be established	Nobody responsible but Banqueting Manager did certain pricing	A Manager should be responsible

AREA/PROCEDURES	COMMENTS FOOD DEPT	RECOMMENDATIONS	COMMENTS BEVERAGE DEPT	RECOMMENDATIONS
2. How often are they revised?	Not known		Not known	Responsibility and system to be established
3. Do selling prices include VAT?	No		No	
L. Controls				
12. Is a diary kept by the Unit Manager?	Yes		Yes	
13. Any record kept of function taken place, if banqueting:				
a) who does the bills?	Banqueting Manager		Banqueting Manager	
14. Are they broken down as:				
a) food?	Yes		Yes	
b) beverage?	Yes		Yes	
wine-drinks?	Yes		Yes	
c) miscellaneous?	Yes		Yes	
15. At agreed prices?	Yes	Duplicate letter of confirmation with prices to be recorded	Yes	Duplicate letter of confirmation with prices to be recorded
16. Are empty bottles kept for customers' verification			Yes	
17. Are there any complaints of overcharging?	Not known	Investigate who receives complaint letters	Not known	Investigate who receives complaint letters
18. Are receipts recorded by cash registers or other-wise?	Receipts are handed to accounts	To be discussed with the Accountant	Receipts are handed to the accounts	To be discussed with the Accountant

AREA/PROCEDURE	COMMENTS FOOD DEPT	RECOMMENDATIONS	COMMENTS BEVERAGE DEPT	RECOMMENDATIONS
19. How are cash functions handled in banqueting?	Banqueting Manager pays in cash the next day	New procedure to be introduced immediately and discussed with Banqueting Manager and Accountant	Banqueting Manager pays in cash next day	New procedure to be introduced immediately and discussed with Banqueting Manager and Accounts
20. Are they numbered and/or duplicated?	All receipts are numbered and duplicated		All receipts are numbered and duplicated	
21. How are overage and shortages handled?	Not known	Discuss with Accountant	Not known	Discuss with Accountant
H. Selling price				
4. Do they include service?	No		No	
5. Do they include room hire?	No		No	
6. Are discontinued selling prices recorded?	No	Start record	No	Start record
I. Statistics				
1. Are any figures of same period of the previous year(s) available?	Only a few due to a lot of changes in the accountancy		Only a few due to a lot of changes in accountanvy	
2. Any comparison figures available for similar establishments?	No		No	
3. Has method of reporting altered?	No		No	
J. Revenue				
1. Cash - recorded on tills?	Yes		Yes	

AREA/PROCEDURES	COMMENTS FOOD DEPT	RECOMMENDATIONS	COMMENTS BEVERAGE DEPT	RECOMMENDATIONS
2. Is there a daily control reconciling cash takings with audit till rolls?	No - sometimes	To be introduced from today	No - sometimes	To be introduced from today
3. Credit -				
a) Are there bills for credit functions?	Yes	Procedure to be devised and discussed with Accountant/ Banqueting Manager	Yes	
b) Are the bills controlled?	No		No	Procedure to be devised and discussed with Accountant/Banqueting Manager
c) Who sends credit bills to customers?	Banqueting Manager		Banqueting Manager	
K. Staffing				
1. Obtain a complete list of personnel		List with job titles		
2. Have any if the staff a special relationship?	None Catering Manager who left was married to Banqueting Secretary		None Catering Manager who left was married to Banqueting Secretary	List with job titles
L. Controls				
1. Are cash registers readings taken daily by an independent person?	Not as a routine, sometimes by the owner	A person must be appointed for this task preferrably from accounts	Not as a routine, sometimes by the owner	A person must be appointed for this task
2. Who is this person?	The owner		The owner	Preferrably from the accounts

AREA/PROCEDURES	COMMENTS FOOD DEPT	RECOMMENDATIONS	COMMENTS BEVERAGE DEPT	RECOMMENDATIONS
3. Who has access to the reading key?	The owner	Only the one who is responsible for reading cash registers		Only the one who is responsible for reading cash registers
4. Are the readings reconciled with cashiers' reports?	No	To be checked by accounts	No	To be checked by accounts
5. Are any daily analysis sheets produced?	Yes	To be continued	Yes	To be continued
6. How are they broken down?				
in a) cash?	Yes		Yes	
b) credit?	Yes		Yes	
c) periods?	Lunch/Dinner daily		Lunch/Dinner daily	
d) individual items?	Food, beverage and tobacco		Food, beverage and tobacco	
e) transfers?	Yes	Transfers preferrably to be avoided but if any to be dealt with properly	Yes	Transfers preferrably to be avoided but if any to be dealt with properly
7. Are voids/cancellations rechecked with counter-signed?	No	By accounts	No	By accounts
8. Are prices checked on bills?	No	By accounts	No	By accounts
9. How are complimentary drinks/meals processed?	No system	Every meal to be signed for and handled as revenue for the day	No system	Every drink has to be signed for and handled as revenue of the day
10. How are they shown in the accounts?	Not shown at all on a regular basis	To be discussed with accounts	Not shown at all on a regular basis	To be discussed with Accountant
11. Does the food and beverage cost of sales fall near the budget?	n/a		n/a	

In the present case, it took the Beverage Controller one day to complete the stocktake and the Food Controller two days. A second stocktake was taken on the following Monday and all results were ready by the Thursday. The results are shown on pages 110–112.

All three outlets show a substantial difference between actual and potential cost. This was largely due to large portions, over-production, poor storage facilities and pilferage.

If we look at the second week's results (on page 111) we can see a considerable improvement in the variance: The overall and individual potential costs remained almost the same. It was then decided to re-cost and re-price all the menu items in outlet three in order to get an overall food cost of forty per cent. The re-costing exercise showed that prices needed to be increased by about ten per cent. The last price increase had taken place ten months before. The price increases were implemented during the third week and their effects showed already by the end of that week. (see page 112)

Bars TB and TRC produced an excellent result, far too good a result in fact. (see page 113) Both bars came under the control of a Banqueting Manager who moved various stock items from one bar to another to produce a better result. He camouflaged this movement of stock by 'losing' transfer dockets and made the excuse that he did not have time to make correct transfers. During the week he bought six cases of cheap, sparkling wine for a function and sold them at a cost of sales of 34%, whereas the normal sparkling wine on the wine list would have a cost of 51.19%. If we take out the cost and revenue relating to this sparkling wine from the results we have an overall cost percentage of 49.8%.

	All Bars				Period 16.10 – 22.10	
	Potential £	%	Actual £	%	Variances £	%
Revenue	1946.24	100	2158.37	100	+212.13	+10.9
Cost	917.14	*47.12	917.13	42.49		– 4.63
Gross profit	1029.11	42.88	1241.24	57.51	+212.13	+ 4.63

Note:* Without the Revenue and Cost for the 67 bottles of sparkling wine the cost percentage would have been 49.8% and part of the high variance was also caused through overcharging customers. Complaints about this were received three weeks later.

Test:			
	1946.24	917.13	47.12%
	– 335.00	–113.90	34%
	1611.24	803.23	49.8%

In bar TW the result was four per cent down on potential because of £27.10 which was accounted for as food revenue rather than beverage revenue and because of cash being mishandled. (see page 114)

All the bar results were discussed with the Bar Manager and the Banqueting Manager at once and all staff were warned that there should not be any repetition of the incidents mentioned above.

It was also decided that draught beer should be discontinued in Bar TRC to cut down wastage. Soda syphons were also removed from all bars and they were replaced by bottles at the same price as other baby minerals.

The overall bar result suggests that the total cost percentage should be around fifty per cent (see page 114) following sales analysis by group of items for each of the three bars and for the three bars together. (see pages 115–116)

A quick cost comparison of each individual product showed if we could combine our purchasing power with this establishment we could reduce the total cost percentage for beverages by fifteen per cent because of better discounts. This would mean a reduction of the overall cost percentage to forty-one per cent and so only a few small price increases would have been necessary. This was, in fact, not possible because the establishment was a 'tied house' and all products had to be bought from a brewery and its subsidiary companies. It was therefore necessary to increase the majority of prices. Our company decided in fact not to purchase this establishment and so these price increases were not made effective until after the period under consideration. They would however have reduced the beverage cost percentage to an acceptable level. The stocktake results for the third week of the exercise show potential and actual to be almost equal but the overall cost percentage to be too high at 48.5%.

Food outlets Period 16.10–22.10

	One		Two		Three		Total		
	Potential	Actual	Potential	Actual	Potential	Actual	Potential	Actual	Variance
Revenue	410.66	378.87	592.40	596.40	1086.28	1086.28	2089.34	2061.55	– 27.79
Cost	171.27	183.49	233.70	265.31	488.83	564.17	893.80	1012.97	+119.17
Cost %	41.7%	48.4%	39.4%	44.5%	45%	51.9%	42.8%	49.1%	+ 6.3 %
% of sale	19.6%		28.4%		52%		100%		

Food outlets Period 23.10–29.10

	One		Two		Three		Total		
	Potential	Actual	Potential	Actual	Potential	Actual	Potential	Actual	Variance
Revenue	349.92	312.44	642.35	638.40	1136.00	1136.00	2128.27	2086.84	–41.43
Cost	143.91	139.80	251.52	264.28	507.79	543.64	903.22	947.72	+44.50
Cost %	41.1%	44.7%	39.17%	41.4%	44.7 %	47.8%	42.4%	45.4%	+ 3 %
% of sale	16.4%		30.2 %		53.4 %		100%		

Food outlets Period 30.10–5.11

	One		Two		Three		Total		
	Potential	Actual	Potential	Actual	Potential	Actual	Potential	Actual	Variance
Revenue	314.19	317.16	499.71	503.41	979.68	979.68	1793.58	1800.25	+6.67
Cost	129.81	130.64	195.88	197.84	402.69	405.84	728.38	734.32	+5.94
Cost %	41.3%	41.2%	39.2%	39.3%	41.1%	41.4%	40.6%	40.8%	+ .2 %
% of sale	17.5%		27.9%		54.6%		100%		

Bar T.B. Period 16.10–22.10

	Potential		Actual		Variances	
Revenue	£709.85	100%	£879.17	100%	£169.32	+23.85%
Cost	£287.56	40.51%	£287.56	32.71%		− 7.8 %
Gross profit	£422.29	59.43%	£591.20	67.25%	+£169.32	+ 7.82%

Note: * Without the revenue and cost of the sixty-seven bottles of sparkling wine the cost percentage would have been 46.3%
The high variance was also caused through overcharging customers. In fact a letter to that effect was received three weeks later.

Test:			
	709.85	287.56	40.51%
	−335.00	−113.90	34%
	374.85	173.66	46.3%

Bar T.R.C. Period 16.10–22.10

	Potential		Actual		Variances	
Revenue	£344.58	100%	£455.79	100%	+£111.21	+32.27%
Cost	£173.05	50.22%	£173.05	37.97%		−12.25%
Gross profit	£171.53	49.78%	£282.74	62.03%	+£111.21	+12.25%

Note: The low cost was due to transfers of various bottles to Bar T.B.

Bar T.W. Period 16.10–22.10

	Potential		Actual		Variances	
Revenue	£891.81	100%	£823.41	100%	−£68.40	−7.67%
Cost	£456.52	51.19%	£456.52	55.44%		+4.25%
Gross profit	£435.29	48.81%	£366.89	44.56%	−£68.40	−4.25%

Note: £27.10 went by mistake into food revenue. The actual result would have been reduced to 53.68%.

Test:

823.41	actual revenue
+ 27.10	
850.51	adjusted revenue
456.52	cost
53.7 %	cost

Record of group returns of bar T.B. 16.10–22.10

Group items	Revenue	Cost	Cost %	% of sales
Aperitifs/Port	33 57	10 86	32.4	4.7
Sherry	— 55	— 22	40.0	0.08
Spirits	142 97	59 28	41.5	20.14
Waters/squashes/juices	48 21	27 24	56.5	6.79
Draught beer	36 68	18 56	50.6	5.20
Bottled beer	— 21	— 11	52.4	0.03
Brandy/liqueurs	14 22	7 87	51.8	2.0
Wines	433 44	163 92	37.8	61.06
Total	709 85	287 56	40.51%	100%

Note: Low percentage figure was due to the sparkling wine.

Test:			
	433 44	163 92	37.8%
	−335 00	−113 90	34 %
	98 44	50 02	50.8%

Record of group returns of bar T.R.C. 16.10–22.10

Group items	Revenue	Cost	Cost %	% of sales
Aperitifs/Port	22 87	8 77	38.3	6.6
Sherry	7 68	2 71	35.3	2.2
Spirits	64 13	27 06	42.2	18.6
Waters/squashes/juices	37 28	16 30	43.7	10.8
Draught beer	68 95	36 40	52.8	20.0
Bottled beer	8 10	3 78	46.7	2.4
Brandy/liqueurs	21 70	11 64	53.6	6.3
Wines	113 87	66 39	58.3	33.1
Total	344 58	173 05	50.22%	100%

Record of group returns of bar T.W. 16.10–22.10

Group items	Revenue	Cost	Cost %	% of sales
Aperitifs/Port	35 69	11 45	32.08	4.0
Sherry	28 93	9 54	32.9	3.3
Spirits	152 75	70 54	46.2	17.1
Waters/squashes/juices	157 39	67 90	43.2	17.6
Draught beer	450 64	257 46	57.1	50.5
Bottled beer	28 39	16 58	58.4	3.2
Brandy/liqueurs	7 74	4 00	51.7	0.9
Wines	30 28	19 05	62.9	3.4
Total	891 81	456 52	51.2 %	100%

All bars 16.10–22.10

Group items	Revenue	Cost	Cost %	% of sales
Aperitifs/Port	92 13	31 03	33.7	4.7
Sherry	37 16	12 47	33.5	1.9
Spirits	359 85	156 88	43.6	18.5
Waters/squashes/juices	242 88	111 44	45.9	12.5
Draught beer	556 27	312 42	56.2	28.6
Bottled beer	36 70	20 47	55.8	1.9
Brandy/liqueurs	43 66	23 01	52.7	2.2
Wines	577 59	249 36	43.2	29.7
Total	1946 24	917 13	47.36%	100%

Note: Price increases of between 8% and 25% are required to reduce the overall cost per cent to 40% provided the same sales analysis is maintained.

Test:			
	577 59	249 36	43.2%
	−335 00	−113 90	34 %
	242 59	135 46	55.8%

All bars Period 30.10–5.11.78

	Potential		Actual		Variances	
Revenue	£2346.48	100%	£2343.01	100%	−£3.47	0.06%
Cost	£1138.98	48.54%	£1138.98	48.6%		−0.1 %
Gross profit	£1207.50	51.46%	£1204.03	51.4%	−£3.47	−0.06%

11 Case study: assessing a planned change from a pub-style bar to a discotheque bar

The first step in this exercise was to gather information about other bar and discotheque operations. We gathered from a variety of other operations the following information.

Classification of hotel: AA listing.
Location of bar, floor level, entrance and ease of access.
Decoration and theme: style, lighting, furniture, continuity of theme.
Size: seating capacity, approximate area, arrangement of facilities.
Service: Bar service, waiter service or mixed.
Food available: full bar, wines or cocktails.
Pricing policies: cover charge, prices for beer, spirits, cocktails, food prices, later night prices, entrance fee.
Entertainment: piano, dancing, discotheque, cabaret, background music, other.
Customers: age, class, sex, tourist/local, popularity rating.
Samples: obtain drinks, menu cards, book matches where possible.

The necessary minimum of revenue needed from the new operation had already been decided by our company board during the initial planning stages. After meticulous planning a price structure was agreed and price increases and decreases (because of the grouping of some items at a standard price) were agreed. These can be seen on the table on page 48.

Using stocktake results it is easy to formulate the projected revenue increase to be expected from sales of particular group and in total. In this case the estimated weekly revenue based on the pattern of business in the old bar was £5 656.74 (see page 118). The budgeted revenue was £8 870 and the actual revenue per week averaged £9 788.75 which is 10.36% over budget. The estimated sales based on the old bar operation were made up of in-house sales to guests at the hotel. The discotheque would obviously attract customers from outside and the budget presumed a 56% increase in business because of this. In fact, business increased by 73%. Market research showed that the split in revenue was 30% in-house and 70% from outside.

The table (page 119) shows how by the end of the third week's trading some of the sales percentages have changed in comparison with those of the old bar operation. As a result, beverage cost was 0.82% higher than expected. By the ninth week (page 120) the cost

Record of group returns: 1 week's analysis old bar

Group items	Total group cost	%Cost	Total sales group	Cost% group	Sales %	Price % Increase per group	% Uplift
Aperitifs	£ 44.13	3.2%	173.36	25.46	3.9	19.7%	4.67
Ports	3.03	0.22%	10.86	27.9	.23	26.1%	0.29
Sherries	8.86	0.64%	32.37	27.37	.72	16.7%	0.84
Gins	144.41	10.49%	530.15	27.24	11.75	22. %	14.34
Scotch whiskies	165.70	12.03%	542.06	30.54	12.20	21.8 %	14.86
Irish whiskies	38.50	2.8%	128.85	29.88	2.9	6.9%	3.1
Rye and Bourbon	19.09	1.4%	58.10	32.86	1.3	7.7%	1.4
Rums	40.40	2.93%	142.17	28.42	3.2	42.56%	4.56
Vodkas	97.55	7.08%	366.79	26.6	8.26	19.0%	9.83
Brandies	52.18	3.79%	159.21	32.77	3.57	-14.8%	3.04
Liqueurs	43.04	3.12%	148.06	29.07	3.3	52.1%	5.02
Wines	25.55	1.86%	61.04	41.86	1.37	-44.5%	0.76
Draught Beers	482.36	35.02%	1295.60	37.23	29.07	41.1%	41.02
Bottled Beers	45.99	3.34%	150.85	30.49	3.29	21.0%	3.98
Waters	161.60	11.73%	624.33	25.88	14.06	27.9%	17.99
Squashes	4.77	0.35%	44.40	10.74	.89	1.1%	0.90
	£1377.16	100%	4468.20	30.8%	100%		126.6

Note The overall average price increase of 26.6% would reduce the cost of sales from 30.8% to 24.35%. Estimated revenue is £5656.74. I imagined that the steep increase in the price of draught beer would reduce the revenue from this item by 50%. If each customer bought a bottled beer instead, however, we could maintain the revenue and improve the cost slightly.

Record of group returns: third week trading analysis of the new bar

Group items	Total group cost	% cost of	Total sales group	Cost % group	Sales %
Aperitifs	£ 93.98	3.6%	£ 424.45	22.14	4.14
Ports	£ 3.98	0.15%	£ 9.91	40.16	0.10
Sherries	£ 4.97	0.2%	£ 14.59	34.06	0.14
Gins	£ 221.34	8.5%	£1037.82	21.33	10.12
Scotch whiskies	£ 372.28	14.3%	£1410.48	26.39	13.75
Irish whiskies	£ 34.13	1.3%	£ 134.37	25.4	1.31
Rye and Bourbon	£ 53.98	2.1%	£ 210.03	25.7	2.05
Rums	£ 98.27	3.8%	£ 417.60	23.53	4.07
Vodkas	£ 209.37	8.02%	£ 988.27	21.19	9.64
Brandies	£ 131.41	5.1%	£ 463.22	28.37	4.52
Liqueurs	£ 148.47	5.72%	£ 623.07	23.83	6.08
Wines	£ 324.59	12.5%	£ 780.02	41.6	7.61
Draught beers	£ 531.95	20.5%	£2079.73	25.58	20.28
Bottled beers	£ 68.13	2.62%	£ 273.64	24.89	2.67
Waters	£ 250.79	9.7%	£1266.92	19.8	12.35
Cigars	£ 34.33	1.30%	£ 44.36	77.39	0.43
Squashes	£ 14.31	0.6%	£ 75.95	18.8	0.74
	£2596.28	100%	£10254.43	25.32	100%

Without cigars 25.17%

Record of group items: 9th week of trading of the new outlet

Group items	Total group cost		Total sales group	Cost % group	Sales %
Aperitifs	£ 71.30	2.92	300.21	23.75	3.1
Ports	4.85	0.2	14.62	33.17	0.15
Sherries	8.15	0.33	33.54	24.3	0.35
Gins	207.70	8.5	966.45	21.49	9.97
Scotch whiskies	208.03	12.61	1210.48	25.45	12.48
Irish whiskies	14.39	0.59	57.59	24.99	0.59
Rye and Bourbon	79.40	3.25	284.61	27.9	2.93
Rums	144.15	5.9	609.66	23.64	6.29
Vodkas	190.69	7.81	909.30	20.97	9.38
Brandies	108.95	4.46	394.57	27.62	4.07
Liqueurs	238.31	9.76	990.10	24.07	10.21
Wines	294.04	12.04	695.82	42.26	7.18
Draught beers	405.41	16.6	1633.86	24.81	16.85
Bottled beers	71.50	2.93	285.69	25.03	2.95
Waters	235.71	9.65	1170.81	20.13	12.07
Cigars	39.38	1.61	47.77	82.44	0.49
Squashes	20.52	0.84	91.09	22.53	0.94
	2442.48	100	9696.17	25.19%	100%

Without cigars 24.9%

percentage had improved to 24.9% but it was still 0.55% short of the cost forecast. This was partly due to cost increases of £86 per week (approximately 3% of total cost) which had not been budgeted. This will of course have a greater or smaller impact on the cost percentage depending on the level of sales.

If we compare the table relating to the old bar operation (page 118) with the table relating to the ninth and third weeks of the new operation (pages 119–20) we find some significant changes in the sales of some of the item groups.

Irish Whiskies – most sold because of the change in clientele.
Ryes andBourbons – more sold because of increased cocktail sales and reasonable pricing.
Rums – more sold because of increased cocktail sales.
Brandies – more sold because of increased cocktail sales and reasonable pricing.
Liqueurs – more sold because of increase cocktail sales.
Wines – more sold because of prices kept low as in the old bar.
Draught beers – reduction of sales as planned.
Cigars – introduced in new bar.

In general, although the actual costs vary slightly from the forecast this was a fairly accurate estimate of sales for the new bar.

If we look closely at our figures for draught and bottled beers (see below) we can demonstrate how very misleading figures can be if they are not used and interpreted with care. Here is a summary of changes in beer sales over the period of the introduction of the new bar operation.

Old bar	**Cost**	**Sales**	**Cost %**	**Sales %**	**Price increases**
Draught beers	482.36	1295.60	37.23%	29.07%	41.1% (page 118)
Bottled beer	45.99	150.85	30.49%	3.29%	21% (page 118)

New bar	**Cost**	**Sales**	**Cost %**	**Sales %**	**Price increases**
Draught beers	531.95	2079.73	25.58%	20.28%	(41.1%) (page 119)
Bottled	68.13	273.64	24.89%	2.67%	(21%) (page 119)

We can see from these figures that, although the price of draught beer was increased by 41.1%, there seems to have been no decrease in the consumption of this beverage. On the contrary, if we subtract the 41.1% due to price increases from new bar sales of £2 079.73 we still have an increase of 13.76% over sales in the old bar. There is also an improvement in the cost percentage of sales of 1.14% which is due to an improved discount deal with the brewery.

First we discount the effect of the 41.1% price increase:

$$\frac{£2079.73 \times 100}{141.1} = £1473.94$$

To find the increase in consumption after subtracting the effect of the price increase we subtract our adjusted figure from the old bar revenue:

£1473.94 − £1295.60 = £178.34 sales increase

We can then express this as a percentage increase on old bar sales:

$$\frac{£178.34 \times 100}{£1295.60} = 13.76\% \text{ adjusted revenue increase}$$

If we compare the cost of sales percentage of the adjusted new bar sales with those of the old we have:

$$\frac{£531.95 \times 100}{£1473.94} = 36.09\%$$

This is a 1.14% improvement on the 37.23% figure for old bar sales.

If we look at bottled beer sales using the same technique we find that sales of bottled beers have increased by 49.9% but the adjusted cost percentage figure remains much the same. This is due to the increased sales of Löwenbräu which was priced quite low.

$$\frac{£273.64 \times 100}{121} = £226.15 \text{ adjusted sales total}$$

£226.15 − £150.85 = £75.30 adjusted sales increase

$$\frac{£75.30 \times 100}{£150.85} = 49.9\% \text{ adjusted sales increase}$$

$$\frac{£68.13 \times 100}{£226.15} = 30.13\% \text{ adjusted cost percentage}$$

This is a 0.36% improvement on the figure for the old bar of 30.49%.

If we combine sales of draught and bottled beers there seems to be an overall increase of 17.5% in sales.

£1295.60 + £150.85 = £1446.45 total sales old bar

£178.34 + £75.30 = £253.64 total increase on old bar sales

$$\frac{£253.64 \times 100}{£1446.45} = 17.5\% \text{ increase on old bar sales}$$

If, finally, we examine the total bar turnover figures using the same principle of adjusted totals it shows an overall increase of 81.3%. First we adjust the new bar turnover to take account of a 26.6% price increase:

$$\frac{£10254.43 \times 100}{126.6} = £8099.86 \text{ adjusted turnover}$$

If we subtract the old bar turnover from this adjusted new bar turnover we can find the adjusted turnover increase.

£8099.80 − £4468.20 = £3631.60 turnover increase

This represents an 81.3% increase in turnover after adjustment.

We can now relate the beer sales figures to the total turnover figures and an interesting picture emerges. In the old bar draught beer accounted for 29.07% of the total sales and bottled beer for 3.29%. This is a total for all beers of 32.36% of a turnover of £4468.20. In the new bar draught beer accounts for 20.28% of the total sales and bottled beer for 2.67%. This is a total of 22.95% of a turnover of £10254.43.

Here we can see a decrease in the share of beer sales of total turnover of 9.41%. If we relate beer sales to the adjusted turnover figures we see an even greater decrease of 11.37%. The adjusted turnover for the new bar is £8099.86. If we express total beer sales as a percentage of this we have

$$\frac{£1700.09 \times 100}{£8099.86} = 20.99\%$$

If we subtract this from the percentage of total sales accounted for by beers in the old bar we have

32.26% − 20.99% = 11.37% real decrease

12 Watch your meat and save money

We have already discussed (page 000) that the following rules are of vital importance in the control of meat.

1 Make sure that meat quality is right when you buy.
2 Make sure that the price is right when you buy.
3 Make sure that meat is weighed on arrival.
4 Make sure that it is stored carefully.
5 Make sure that meat is cut and trimmed to standard.

There is one other important element in the control of loss. This is the cooking temperature, which should be about 300°F. Below are the comparisons of weight loss of a few meat items when they are cooked at low and high temperatures.

Items	Low (300°F)	High (430°F)	Bone loss
Rib of beef	20%	30%	20%
Sirloin of beef	20%	30%	20%
Topside	18%	30%	–
Pork, leg	15%	20%	10%
Veal, leg	20%	30%	20%
Lamb, leg	15%	20%	10%

Your chef should do these exercises. If this principle is followed your meat consumption will decrease. The chef should also do random comparisons of meat deliveries to check their quality and composition. On page 125 are four examples:

	SCOTCH SIRLOIN		ENGLISH SIRLOIN		RUMP	
	Ratio	Gross Weight	Ratio	Gross Weight	Ratio	Gross Weight
	100%	21 lbs	100%	25 lbs	100%	30 lb
Fat	11.9%	2 lbs 8 ozs	14½%	3 lbs 10 ozs	17½%	5 lbs 4 ozs
Bones	20%	4 lbs 3 ozs	19%	4 lbs 12 ozs	16.7%	5 lbs
Trimmings	16.4%	3 lbs 7 ozs	18½%	4 lbs 10 ozs	12½%	3 lbs 12 ozs
Fillet	7.1%	1 lb 8 ozs	7½%	1 lb 14 ozs	6.7%	2 lbs
Sirloin (net)	44.6%	9 lbs 6 ozs	40½%	10 lbs 2 ozs	46.6%	14 lbs
Cooking loss (25%)		2 lbs 6 ozs		2½ lbs		3½ lbs
Meat cooked (75%)		7 lbs		7 lbs 13 ozs		10½ lbs

	LEG OF VEAL	
	Ratio	Gross Weight
	100%	50 lbs
Fat	8%	4 lbs
Bones	13.25%	6 lbs 10 ozs
Trimming	6.75%	3 lbs 6 ozs
Knuckle	12%	6 lbs
Meat (net)	60%	30 lbs

13 Pricing policy

The selling price of a dish depends mainly on the quality offered, the cost of materials, wages costs, all other overhead expenses and, of course, VAT. The average customer spend on a meal can vary considerably depending on the menu available and on the customer's decision to spend more or less each time they come into the restaurant. When the customer leaves after his meal, if he has spent more than he intended, will probably not return.

The price structure of a menu must be correctly balanced. The correct balance is arrived at by considering the following factors.

1 The right selection of items must be offered to the customer.
2 The price must be acceptable to him.
3 Each group of dishes should have a range of prices starting with the lowest. In general, though, the highest price should not be more than three times the lowest.
4 There should not be any large fluctuations of price in each group of dishes.
5 You should keep a record of the choices that the customer actually makes at all times.
6 Remember that most customers evaluate a restaurant by adding up prices.

I will now show a method of calculating average prices and average spend. In the first group of dishes there are nine items. The total price of these nine items is £11.95. In a certain period 917 items were sold and the total revenue was £1021.45. From this we can calculate:

1 The average price offered to the customer

$$\frac{\text{£}11.95}{9 \text{ items}} = \text{£}1.3277$$

2 The average price paid by the customer

$$\frac{\text{£}1021.45}{917} = \text{£}1.1139$$

3 The ratio of the two averages

$$\frac{1.1139 \quad \text{(average spend)}}{1.3277 \quad \text{(average offered)}} = 0.84$$

The best ratio falls between 0.7 and 0.9. If the ratio is greater than 0.9 this is an indication that items at a lower price are not being chosen by customers. In this case one should introduce a higher-priced dish or discontinue the least popular lower-priced dishes. If the ratio is less than 0.7 the reverse is true and cheaper dishes are selling in larger quantities than the more expensive ones. In either case one should change the menu grouping in such a way that the sales pattern results in the best ratio. On page 128 is an exercise which compares revenue figures and sales patterns for two years.

As we can see the numbers of starters and main courses sold dropped considerably because of the introduction of a very low priced table d'hôte menu to attract more customers and boost revenue. This may seem at first sight to have been a correct decision because the average spend per cover increased to £3.05. There was also, though, a new lounge service introduced where all the menu items were served. In order to make a fair comparison the revenue must also be included. Here are the present year's figures amended:

No of codes	Total dishes served	Menu prices (excl VAT)	Total revenue (excl VAT)	Ratios
		£	£	%
9	723	13.67	884.94	–
20	1637	69.79	5183.29	–
17	2254	21.33	1640.41	–
	1005		777.00	–
		1.5188	1.2239	0.80
		3.4895	3.1663	0.91
		1.2547	0.7417	0.59

Covers increased from 2528 to 3533

Thus the adjusted average spending on food is only £2.40 per person – a decrease of 5.7% compared to last year. The menu composition and price structure was slightly adjusted in the present year in order to achieve the ideal ratios but, as you can see, the ratios are still not right. In general the decreases in food revenue were caused by economic recession, by the introduction of the low-priced menu and the introduction of the new regulations contained in the *Price Marking Order 1979 (Food and Drink on Premises)*. This demanded the inclusion of VAT at fifteen per cent in all menu prices. Previously all menu items were advertised exclusive of the lower rate (8%) of VAT. Customers were, therefore, encouraged to choose cheaper dishes under the new regulations. It is also apparent from the analysis above that the introduction of a low priced table d'hôte menu encouraged customers to buy more liquor items.

	Last year					Present year				
	No of codes	Total dishes sold	Menu prices (excl VAT) offered	Total revenue	Ratios	No of codes sold	Total dishes sold	Menu prices (excl VAT) offered	Total revenue	Ratios
Starters	9	917	£11.95	£1021.45		9	723	£13.67	£ 884.94	
Main courses	19	1803	£59.45	£5458.15		20	1637	£69.79	£5183.29	
Hot bev/light ref/sweets	17	3520	£28.40	£2248.20		17	2254	£21.33	£1640.41	
			1.3277	1.1139	0.84			1.5188	1.2239	0.80
			3.1289	3.0272	0.97			3.4898	3.1663	0.91
			1.6705	0.6386	0.38			1.2547	0.7277	0.58
	No of sleepers 7393		Total covers 3428			No of sleepers 7241		Total covers 2528		
	Average spend per sleeper			£1.18 on food		Average spend per sleeper			£1.06 on food	
	Average spend per cover			£2.55 on food		Average spend per cover			£3.05 on food	
	Average spend per sleeper			15.8p on beverage		Average spend per sleeper			17p on beverage	
	Average spend per cover			34p on beverage		Average spend per cover			49p on beverage	

Notes:
1 The number of sleepers decreased by 2.05%
2 The sleeper spending on food decreased by 10.17%
3 The spending per cover seems to have increased on food by 19.6% but if you look to the realistic comparison figures (see page 127) it decreased by 5.7% which does not include price increases over that period.
4 The sleeper spending on beverages increased by 7.6%
5 The beverage spend per cover increased by 44.1%

14 Computing and food and beverage control

One of the biggest problems in any manual system of food and beverage control is the length of time taken to produce the complete and usable information which a manager needs. In very few cases are figures available within a few days. In my case controllers produce figures for six outlets up to the close of business on Sunday, at the following speeds:

Beverages – actual and potential figures on Tuesday evening.
Food – potential figures on Tuesday evening.
Food – actual figures on Wednesday evening.

Although this is fairly fast, if there are any discrepancies three or four days have been lost before they can be investigated and the problem isolated. It is, therefore, obvious that a rapid, computerised system can give tremendous advantages. Such a system would allow information to be gathered on a daily basis or even after each session of business. Discrepancies can then be investigated and rectified immediately.

The viability of a computerised system depends very much on the size of an establishment. It is not, however, always necessary or desirable to automate all functions in food and beverage outlets. There is, in fact, a danger of computerising too many functions. The manager must consider which specific functions warrant automation. Systems which would seem to warrant computerisation are sales and menu analysis and, perhaps, requisitioning, receiving, inventory detail and the issues and transfers of products and menu items.

Menu explosion

Menu explosion is a vital part of food and beverage control. Ingredients can be fed into the system and potential costs can be calculated on a daily or other period basis. Potential costs can then be compared to actual costs derived from actual usage. The differences between the two can highlight theft, spoilage or the incurrence of unexpected costs.

The other part of menu explosion is the evaluation of the effects of price increases or menu changes on revenue and profit. A computer-aided system allows the food and beverage manager to do this.

The cash register

Sophisticated, pre-programmed cash registers can be linked to the computer and can record the number of portions of individual menu items which have been sold. If this system is too expensive, however, such a sales analysis can be input manually into the computer. To speed up service procedures a cash register can be linked to a remote printer in the kitchen, or dispense bar. How such a system might be arranged depends of course on the order and billing system in use.

Potential control

As mentioned above a key part of control is the comparison of the volume of goods entering the establishment with the reported volume of goods consumed. The system works back from reported sales which are exploded into ingredients and compared with actual consumption of the ingredients. Although attempts have been made to estimate sales from reported issues this system is generally less reliable. The same issued item may be used in a variety of menu items and valued differently. In working back however this problem is overcome.

Stocks, issues and inventories

Inventories could be maintained in the nominal ledger as separate accounts for liquor, dry goods, par stocks etc. All invoices relating to these accounts should be posted as addiction in amount only. At periodic intervals a physical inventory should be taken to establish the value of stock. Transfers from one inventory to another would be posted as credits. All sales outlet inventories would be adjusted by the potential cost of sales which is derived from a menu explosion. If any discrepancies are noted between the stock value, reduced by potential cost, and the physical count it can be quickly investigated and analysed in detail. This requires an analysis of the items issued as consumed and can be done accurately.

Bought ledger

The supplier, invoice number, date, amounts, terms and nominal ledger account code are entered into the bought ledger for all purchases. This is a batch process and ensures that the expenses balance to the invoice totals. At the end of the month the distribution is summarised and transferred to the nominal ledger. In the event of a change being made to a balance sheet detail the system requires a short description of the transaction. It is, in this way, possible to print audit statement of changes to capital accounts. All transactions are printed out daily as audit trials for system security.

Selection of a system

The selection of an automated system is not a simple task, especially with the wide range of computing systems now available. The main points to consider when selecting a system are:

1 You must first analyse carefully the needs of your operation.
2 Talk to an impartial computer consultant.
3 Try to look at a system which is already operational.
4 Specify your requirements under three headings – musts, additional wants and likes.
5 Ask computer systems representatives for their suggestions.
6 Compare any suggestion with those of at least three other organisations.
7 Establish carefully the direct, indirect and ongoing cost of a system.
8 Select a system.
9 Draft a contract.
10 Make plans for the introduction of the system.

The major factor is, of course, the final cost of the software and hardware which make up the system. Staff quality is also very important. The effectiveness of a system is very closely related to the quality of the staff using it. No system will compensate for shortcomings in your operation. In a well run organisation a computer system should be regarded as a means of monitoring and improving performance. In a badly run establishment it may be used as an excuse for any kind of problem.

Hotel accountants and computer systems

A recent survey conducted by the British Association of Hotel Accountants shows that:

1 accuracy (1)
2 timeliness (2)
3 reliability (4)

were considered to be of vital importance by over seventy per cent of respondents. The following criteria were rated to be of only average importance:

4 ease of use (3)
5 running costs (6)
6 cost of set up (6)
7 potential staff saving (5)

In my view the order of importance ought to be that indicated by the figures in brackets. Another question was 'How did you, or will you, arrive at your choice of computing solutions?' The answers were:

internal appraisal	70% response
specialist consultant	27%

reference to your existing supplier of computing facilities	18%
recommendation of other users within the industry	25%
no answer	15%

33% of the sample used only one method.
25% used two methods.
10% used three methods.
3% *only* used all four methods.

In answer to a question asking managers to place, in order of importance, key areas of management and control information, food and beverage information on volume and price was placed second.

Fifty five per cent of all managers felt that they were not making adequate use of modern technology. Of those with access to a computer facility, fifty per cent felt that they were not making full use of it.

The question remains, if accuracy is vital, how accurate are present systems? I believe that systems are only fully accurate if the manager knows both the potential *and* actual performance of the business.

Microcomputers

The very recent developments in micro-computerisation made me look for a suitable microcomputer, which not only promises but actually performs the functions I have written about in this book. This small, but powerful, microcomputer system has been programmed with my manual beverage control system. With its relatively low price it could easily be afforded by small businesses in order to improve management and staff performance as well as beverage stock control. The intergrated cellar stock, bar stock, cellar and bar accounting system was developed to meet the needs of most operations and because of its versatility and flexibility it can be adapted by *one bar* operations or up to ten bar outlets – still at a very low price compared to a sophisticated computer system presently still beyond the reach of many hotel and catering establishments.

The system is designed to cut the clerical work involved in keeping an accurate stock record of the cellars, accounting for all goods received, returned or issued to the various bars or departments and the preparation of the beverage control analysis with consolidated results. The system also provides additional information, such as departmental stock valuations, period cost changes as a percentage for each individual item, low stock level warnings and other calculations that would be too time consuming to perform regularly with a normal system.

The following pages show a complete computerised single bar stock report identically to the manual version shown on pages 27 to 35 but with an additional column of stock values incorporated. They also include various reports, analyses, summary reports and a cocktail costing with reference to the similar corresponding manual versions shown on page 53.

The typical manual routine procedure for this particular bar was as follows:–

Manual system	Time	Computer system
1 Preparation of photo copies	10 minutes	Not needed. Stock take sheets printed in 3 minutes.
2 Transfer of closing stock	15 minutes	Automatic transfer
3 To enter on sheets: requisitions tranfers cost changes	 10 minutes	Intergrated automatic transfers and changes
4 Extension of all figures and summaries	2 hours	Automatic
5 Stock evaluation	30 minutes	,, ,,
6 Stocktake time	45 minutes	45 minutes
7 To record closing stock figures	During stocktake	During stocktake
8 To enter total stock figures	After stocktake 5 minutes	After stocktake 12 minutes
Total time needed	4 hours	1 hour

Provided that there are no complications, such as further investigations of inconsistencies or retaking stocks, this timesaving means I have the stock result ready for seven or more outlets on the same day of stocktake. This leaves the controller free from the more routine and time-consuming daily manual functions which gives one the guarantee of improving the cost control because *potential and actuals can be monitored and compared far more accurately and speedily*. It will allow him the opportunity of concentrating more on other costs and expenses, ie with a small additional program, one can easily include in the computerised control system the control of items such as,

1 Non food items (cleaning materials etc)
2 Cutlery, crockery, glasses
3 Spare parts
4 Wages/salary

On the following pages are samples of the microcomputer output based on this control system.

ITEM	OZS	OUTS	STOCK	TOTAL ISSUES	CLOS. STOCK	USAGE	UNIT COST	TOTAL COST	ACTUAL RETAIL	IND COST	POT. SALES	% OF SALES	STOCK VALUE
APERITIFS													
Dubonnet Red	26.40	10.56	1.30	1.00	1.70	0.60	1.91	1.15	7.71	24.77	4.63	0.34	3.25
Dubonnet Dry	26.40	10.56	0.00	0.00	0.00	0.00	1.91	0.00	7.71	24.77	0.00	0.00	0.00
Martini Dry	26.40	10.56	1.80	0.00	1.20	0.60	1.99	1.19	7.71	25.81	4.63	0.34	2.39
Martini Bianco	26.40	10.56	1.50	0.00	1.30	0.20	1.91	0.38	7.71	24.77	1.54	0.11	2.48
Martini Rosso	26.40	10.56	1.60	0.00	1.20	0.40	1.91	0.76	7.71	24.77	3.08	0.22	2.29
Cinzano Bianco	26.40	10.56	0.00	0.00	0.00	0.00	1.81	0.00	7.71	23.48	0.00	0.00	0.00
Campari	26.40	21.12	0.80	1.00	1.60	0.20	4.65	0.93	16.53	28.13	3.31	0.24	7.44
Pernod	24.50	19.60	1.30	0.00	1.30	0.00	5.38	0.00	15.68	34.31	0.00	0.00	6.99
								4.42		25.70	17.18	1.25	24.84
PORTS													
Taylors Ruby	24.64	9.86	1.50	0.00	1.50	0.00	2.36	0.00	6.86	34.40	0.00	0.00	3.54
								0.00		0.00	0.00	0.00	3.54
SHERRIES													
San Angelo		9.86	1.70	0.00	1.40	0.30	1.91	0.57	6.86	27.84	2.06	0.15	2.67
San Carlo		9.86	1.00	1.00	1.70	0.30	1.91	0.57	6.86	27.84	2.06	0.15	3.25
San Dorado		9.86	1.50	0.00	1.20	0.30	1.91	0.57	6.86	27.84	2.06	0.15	2.29
Bristol Cream	26.64	9.86	1.10	1.00	1.60	0.50	2.26	1.13	7.63	29.62	3.82	0.28	3.62
Tio Pepe	26.64	9.86	1.90	0.00	1.90	0.00	2.43	0.00	7.63	31.85	0.00	0.00	4.62
								2.85		28.50	10.00	0.73	16.45
GINS													
Cork Dry		21.12	1.70	0.00	1.70	0.00	4.60	0.00	17.26	26.65	0.00	0.00	7.82
Burne Turner		32.00	2.00	1.00	1.60	1.40	6.67	9.34	26.16	25.50	36.62	2.66	10.67
Gordons	25.66	21.12	0.00	1.00	1.00	0.00	4.60	0.00	17.26	26.65	0.00	0.00	4.60
								9.34		25.50	36.62	2.66	23.09
SCOTCH WHISKY													
Mackinlays		32.00	1.20	1.00	1.30	0.90	7.50	6.75	26.16	28.67	23.54	1.71	9.75
Bells	26.66	21.33	0.50	2.00	1.50	1.00	5.06	5.06	17.43	29.03	17.43	1.26	7.59
								11.81		28.82	40.97	2.97	17.34
IRISH WHISKY													
Paddy	25.40	21.12	1.40	0.00	1.00	0.40	5.00	2.00	19.47	25.68	7.79	0.56	5.00
Jameson	25.40	21.12	1.00	1.00	1.80	0.20	5.00	1.00	19.47	25.68	3.89	0.28	9.00
								3.00		25.68	11.68	0.85	14.00
RYE & BOURBON													
Canadian Club	26.66	21.33	1.80	0.00	1.70	0.10	5.81	0.58	20.40	28.48	2.04	0.15	9.08
Old Crow	26.40	21.12	1.20	0.00	1.20	0.00	5.57	0.00	20.20	27.57	0.00	0.00	6.68
								0.58		28.48	2.04	0.15	16.56

RUMS													
Barcadi		21.33	1.20	0.00	0.40	0.80	5.44	4.35	17.43	31.21	13.94	1.01	2.18
Captain Morgan		21.33	1.20	0.00	1.10	0.10	5.48	0.55	17.43	31.44	1.74	0.13	6.03
								4.90		31.24	15.69	1.14	8.20
VODKAS													
Huzzasr	40.00	32.00	1.00	1.00	0.60	1.40	6.37	8.92	26.16	24.35	36.62	2.66	3.82
								8.92		24.35	36.26	2.66	3.82
BRANDIES													
Armagnac	24.00	19.20	1.00	0.00	1.00	0.00	5.69	0.00	22.59	25.19	0.00	0.00	5.69
Polignac	24.00	19.20	0.30	2.00	1.40	0.90	6.84	6.16	22.54	30.35	20.29	1.47	9.58
Remy Martin	24.00	19.20	1.20	0.00	1.10	0.10	10.34	1.03	30.89	33.47	3.09	0.22	11.37
								7.19		30.76	23.38	1.70	26.64
DRAUGHT BEER													
Harp Larger	GAL		2.00	44	22.00	24.00	2.32	55.68	5.98	38.80	143.52	10.41	51.04
Carlsberg Lager	GAL		11.00	0	0.00	11.00	1.87	20.57	5.98	31.27	65.78	4.77	0.00
Guiness	GAL		11.00	0	10.50	0.50	2.85	1.43	5.98	47.66	2.99	0.22	29.93
								77.68		36.59	212.29	15.40	80.97
BOTTLED BEER													
Carlsberg	BOTT		59	48	48	59.00	1.79	8.80	5.74	31.18	28.22	2.05	7.16
Guiness	BOTT		35	0	32	3.00	2.26	0.57	5.74	39.37	1.44	0.10	6.03
Harp	BOTT		23	0	23	0.00	1.32	0.00	5.74	23.00	0.00	0.00	2.53
Lowenbraw	BOTT		40	72	31	81.00	4.79	32.33	10.96	43.70	73.98	5.37	12.37
Pale Ale	BOTT		43	72	69	46.00	2.00	7.67	5.74	34.84	22.00	1.60	11.50
Cider	BOTT		29	48	46	31.00	2.53	6.54	3.65	69.32	9.43	0.68	9.70
								55.90		41.39	135.07	9.80	49.29
WATERS													
Minerals	BOTT		389	192	455	126.00	0.65	6.83	2.61	24.90	27.41	1.99	24.65
Juices	BOTT		132	276	193	215.00	0.92	16.48	3.65	25.21	65.40	4.74	14.80
7-UP	BOTT		25	96	47	74.00	1.41	8.70	3.65	38.63	22.51	1.63	5.52
Coca-Cola	BOTT		20	72	56	36.00	1.33	3.99	3.65	36.44	10.95	0.79	6.21
Vichi Water	BOTT		28.00	24.00	39.00	13.00	1.95	2.11	6.26	31.15	6.78	0.49	6.34
Pepsi Dr	GALL		0.00	12.38	3.00	9.38	1.38	12.94	7.30	18.90	68.44	4.96	4.14
Lemonade Dr	GALL		4.13	7.25	9.25	2.13	1.25	2.66	7.30	17.12	15.51	1.13	11.56
Perrabelle	BOTT		10.00	0.00	8.00	2.00	1.10	0.18	6.26	17.57	1.04	0.08	0.73
Perrier	BOTT		65	24	30	59.00	2.10	10.33	6.26	33.55	30.78	2.23	5.25
								64.21		25.81	248.81	18.05	79.19
SQUASHES													
Blackcurrant	BOTT		1.40	0.00	0.10	1.30	0.37	0.48	2.61	14.18	3.39	0.25	0.04
Lemon	BOTT		3.00	0.00	3.90	- 0.90	0.32	- 0.29	2.61	12.26	- 2.35	- 0.17	1.25
Lime	BOTT		2.60	1.00	1.50	2.10	0.37	0.78	3.26	11.35	6.85	0.50	0.56
Orange	BOTT		1.80	2.00	4.00	- 0.20	0.37	- 0.07	3.26	11.35	- 0.65	- 0.05	1.48
Peppermint	BOTT		0.20	0.00	0.20	0.00	0.37	0.00	3.26	11.35	0.00	0.00	0.07
Grenadine	BOTT		0.50	0.00	0.50	0.00	1.07	0.00	3.26	32.82	0.00	0.00	0.54
								0.90		12.58	7.24	0.53	3.93

LIQUEURS													
Baileys Irish	24.00	19.70	0.10	0.00	0.10	0.00	4.10	0.00	23.14	17.72	0.00	0.00	0.41
Benedictine	24.34	18.67	0.60	0.00	0.60	0.00	7.36	0.00	21.92	33.58	0.00	0.00	4.42
Cherry Brandy	24.00	19.20	0.60	0.00	0.60	0.00	5.27	0.00	22.54	23.38	0.00	0.00	3.16
Cointreau	24.00	19.20	0.60	0.00	0.40	0.20	6.62	1.32	22.54	29.37	4.51	0.33	2.65
Cr De Menthe	24.00	19.68	0.10	0.00	0.10	0.00	4.81	0.00	23.10	20.82	0.00	0.00	0.4
Drambuie	24.66	18.93	0.40	0.00	0.10	0.30	6.72	2.02	22.22	30.24	6.67	0.48	0.67
Grand Marnier	23.44	18.75	0.90	0.00	0.90	0.00	7.85	0.00	22.01	35.67	0.00	0.00	7.07
Irish Mist		19.20	0.20	0.00	0.20	0.00	6.19	0.00	22.54	27.46	0.00	0.00	1.24
Tia Maria	24.66	19.73	0.70	0.00	0.00	0.70	6.10	4.27	23.16	26.34	16.21	1.18	0.00
Waterford Cream		19.71	0.60	0.00	0.60	0.00	3.42	0.00	23.14	14.78	0.00	0.00	2.05
								7.61		27.79	27.39	1.99	22.14
WINES													
Mercier	BOTT		3.00	2.00	4.00	1.00	5.55	5.55	11.61	47.80	11.61	0.84	22.20
Mercier	1/2		2.00	2.00	3.00	1.00	2.93	2.93	6.30	46.51	6.30	0.46	8.79
Veuve du Vernay	BOTT		4.00	0.00	2.00	2.00	2.19	4.38	5.43	40.37	10.86	0.79	4.38
CH Guineau	BOTT		7.00	0.00	5.00	2.00	2.43	4.86	6.52	37.27	13.04	0.95	12.15
CH Cour d'argent	BOTT		9.00	0.00	9.00	0.00	2.34	0.00	6.78	34.51	0.00	0.00	21.06
CH Panigon	BOTT		10.00	0.00	10.00	0.00	2.76	0.00	6.61	41.75	0.00	0.00	27.60
CH Panigon	1/2		8.00	0.00	7.00	1.00	1.45	1.45	3.43	42.27	3.43	0.25	10.15
Belair Sauvignon	BOTT		5.00	2.00	5.00	2.00	1.69	3.38	5.09	33.20	10.18	0.74	8.45
Belair Sauvignon	1/2		9.00	0.00	9.00	0.00	0.98	0.00	2.83	34.63	0.00	0.00	8.82
Sauternes	BOTT		6.00	0.00	6.00	0.00	2.40	0.00	6.22	38.59	0.00	0.00	14.40
Sauternes	1/2		5.00	4.00	9.00	0.00	1.30	0.00	3.30	39.39	0.00	0.00	11.70
Rose D'Anjou	BOTT		7.90	4.00	10.10	1.80	1.50	2.70	5.09	29.47	9.16	0.66	15.15
Rose D'Anjou	1/2		7.00	3.00	9.00	1.00	0.83	0.83	2.83	29.33	2.83	0.21	7.47
Belair Claret	BOTT		11.00	8.00	12.00	7.00	1.81	12.67	5.09	35.56	35.63	2.58	21.72
Belair Claret	1/2		12.00	4.00	11.00	5.00	0.96	4.80	2.83	33.92	14.15	1.03	10.56
Senators	BOTT		5.00	11.00	6.00	10.00	1.48	14.80	5.09	29.08	50.90	3.69	8.88
Senators	1/2		6.00	5.00	7.20	3.80	0.77	2.93	2.83	27.21	10.75	0.78	5.54
Blanc de Blancs	BOTT		6.00	8.00	7.00	7.00	1.42	9.94	5.09	27.90	35.63	2.58	9.94
Blanc de Blancs	1/2		7.00	5.00	9.00	3.00	0.87	2.61	2.83	30.74	8.49	0.62	7.83
Macon Rouge	BOTT		7.00	4.00	7.00	4.00	1.81	7.24	5.83	31.05	23.32	1.69	12.67
Macon Rouge	1/2		9.00	3.00	9.00	3.00	0.98	2.94	3.22	30.43	9.66	0.70	8.82
Beaujolais	BOTT		8.00	8.00	9.00	7.00	1.89	13.23	5.87	32.20	41.09	2.98	17.01
Beaujolais	1/2		7.00	4.00	5.00	6.00	1.02	6.12	3.26	31.29	19.56	1.42	5.10
Macon Blanc	BOTT		5.00	6.00	7.00	4.00	2.38	9.52	6.70	35.52	26.80	1.94	16.66
Macon Blanc	1/2		3.00	4.00	7.00	0.00	1.23	0.00	3.48	35.34	0.00	0.00	8.61
Mateus Rose	BOTT		4.00	5.00	6.00	3.00	1.97	5.91	5.22	37.74	15.66	1.14	11.82
Mateus Rose	1/2		4.00	3.00	7.00	0.00	1.16	0.00	2.93	40.99	0.00	0.00	8.12
Lutomer Riesling	BOTT		6.00	0.00	5.00	1.00	1.49	1.49	4.48	33.26	4.48	0.32	7.45
Lutomer Riesling	1/2		7.00	4.00	9.00	2.00	0.87	1.74	2.57	33.85	5.14	0.37	7.83
Piesporter	BOTT		5.00	2.00	4.00	3.00	2.35	7.05	6.00	39.17	18.00	1.31	9.40
Piesporter	1/2		7.00	3.00	8.00	2.00	1.04	2.08	3.17	32.81	6.34	0.46	8.32
Goldemer Oktober	BOTT		2.00	10.00	7.00	5.00	1.85	9.25	5.48	33.76	27.40	1.99	12.95
Goldemer Oktober	1/2		7.00	6.00	9.00	4.00	1.05	4.20	3.00	35.00	12.00	0.87	9.45
Oppenheimer	BOTT		4.00	4.00	7.00	1.00	1.74	1.74	5.48	31.75	5.48	0.40	12.18
Oppenheimer	1/2		8.00	0.00	7.00	1.00	0.97	0.97	3.00	32.33	3.00	0.22	6.79
Julien Damov Red	BOTT		9.60	6.00	10.00	5.60	1.60	8.96	6.09	26.27	34.10	2.47	16.00
Julien Damov WH.	BOTT		5.80	18.00	10.90	12.90	1.60	20.64	6.09	26.27	78.56	5.70	17.44
								176.91		31.96	553.56	40.16	433.42
								436.20		31.64	1378.54	100.00	823.44

SUMMARY

POTENTIAL SALES	1378.54		
BREAKAGE AND ULLAGE	- 15.75		
DRINKS TRANSFERES	9.09		
TRANSFERS	0.00		
FINAL POTENTIAL REVENUE	1371.88		
ACTUAL REVENUE	1358.22		
VARIANCE	- 13.66		
COST	436.20		
COST OF FRUIT	0.00		
TOTAL COST INC. FRUIT	436.20		
POTENTIAL COST % EXC FRUIT	31.80	ACTUAL	32.12
POTENTIAL COST % INC FRUIT	31.80	ACTUAL	32.12

WEEKLY BAR SUMMARY REPORT

WEEK 1: BAR: ALL

SUMMARY FOR BAR: ALL

GROUPS:		T.COST	RETAIL	COST %	% SALE
APERITIFS		52.92	217.52	24.33	1.62
SHERRIES		17.04	17.66	96.49	.13
SCOTCH		376.31	1319.45	28.52	9.85
RYE/BOURB.		75.64	225.70	33.51	1.68
VODKAS		170.74	813.00	21.00	6.07
LIQUEURS		194.24	586.87	33.10	4.38
WATERS		432.34	1666.81	25.94	12.44
BEERS		772.22	2348.71	32.88	17.53
CIGARS		43.88	49.56	88.54	.37
PORTS		24.97	18.76	133.10	.14
GINS		208.89	882.12	23.68	6.58
IRISH		21.61	103.62	20.86	.77
RUMS		121.83	490.84	24.82	3.66
BRANDIES		122.76	396.48	30.96	2.96
JUICES		145.15	816.20	17.78	6.09
SQUASHES		27.33	88.94	30.73	.66
WINES		990.66	2759.01	35.91	20.59
MINIATURES		207.38	599.18	34.61	4.47
	FRUIT:	239.15			
	TOTALS:	4245.06	13400.43	31.68	100.00

PERIOD SUMMARY REPORT
BAR: ALL

BAR	ACTUAL	POTENTIAL	VARIANCE	% VAR ACT	COST	% ACT	% POT	% SALE
ONE	20881.52	20089.16	792.36	3.79	6234.91	29.86	31.04	36.8
TWO	9769.19	8486.32	1282.87	13.13	2748.96	28.14	32.39	17.2
THREE	5479.17	5511.08	31.91 -	.58-	1887.15	34.44	34.24	9.6
FOUR	12901.52	12662.89	238.63	1.85	4087.08	31.68	32.28	22.7
FIVE	4331.40	4505.44	174.04 -	4.02-	1541.77	35.60	34.22	7.6
SIX	3339.23	3371.06	31.83 -	.95-	1175.39	35.20	34.87	5.8
TOTAL	56702.03	54625.95	2076.08	3.66	17675.26	31.17	32.36	100.0
FRUIT					777.65	1.37	1.42	

WEEKLY BAR SUMMARY REPORT

WEEK 1: BAR: ONE

SUMMARY FOR BAR: ONE

GROUPS:		T.COST	RETAIL	COST %	% SALE
APERITIFS		.00	.00	.00	.00
SHERRIES		.28-	.67	41.79	.05
SCOTCH		32.56	70.78	46.00	5.58
RYE/BOURB.		8.41	19.60	42.91	1.54
VODKAS		.00	.00	.00	.00
LIQUEURS		.00	.00	.00	.00
WATERS		105.03	354.33	29.64	27.92
BEERS		105.50	284.68	37.06	22.43
PORTS		.00	.00	.00	.00
GINS		9.47	22.76	41.61	1.79
IRISH		.00	.00.	.00	.00
RUMS		5.92	13.39	44.21	1.06
BRANDIES		1.05	2.42	43.39	.19
JUICES		6.74	34.42	19.58	2.71
SQUASHES		.26	2.13	12.21	.17
WINES		94.81	250.94	37.78	19.78
MINIATURES		71.06	214.17	33.18	16.88
	FRUIT:	3.12			
	TOTALS:	443.65	1268.95	34.96	100.00

SUMMARY BAR ONE

POTENTIAL SALES	1268.95		
BREAKAGE AND ULLAGE	00.00		
DRINKS TRANSFERES	59.40		
TRANSFERS	00.00		
FINAL POTENTIAL REVENUE	1209.55		
ACTUAL REVENUE	1160.26		
VARIANCE	- 49.29		
COST	440.53		
COST OF FRUIT	3.12		
TOTAL COST INC. FRUIT	443.65		
POTENTIAL COST % EXC FRUIT	36.42	ACTUAL	37.97
POTENTIAL COST % INC FRUIT	36.68	ACTUAL	38.24

Some mathematical functions are as follows:-

1. $\frac{\text{5.60 (Cost per bottle) x 0.83 (1/6 gill measure)}}{\text{26.67 (bottle content)}}$ = 0.174 cost per measure

2. $\frac{\text{0.70 (Selling price per measure inclusive of VAT x 32 (measures per bottle) x 0.83 (1/6 gill measure x 100 (excl VAT)}}{\text{26.67 (bottle content) x (inclusive 15\% VAT)}}$ = 0.606

3. $\frac{\text{0.174 (Cost per measure) x 100}}{\text{0.606 (retail price per measure excl VAT)}}$ = 28.71% (cost per 1 measure)

4. $\frac{\text{2.30 (Sale price inclusive VAT) x 100}}{\text{115 (inclusive of 15\% VAT)}}$ = (Excl of VAT sale price)

5. $\frac{\text{0.46 (Total cost of cocktail) x 100}}{\text{2.00 (excl VAT sale price)}}$ = 23.00% (actual cost%)

6.
2.00	(Exclusive VAT actual sale price)
-1.815	(Exclusive VAT recommended sale price based on recipe)
0.185	(Exclusive VAT plus revenue obtained for every cocktail served)

DATE: 24.10.79 BAR:ONE

COCKTAIL NAME: SINGAPORE GIN SLING

	INGREDIENTS	OZS	OZ/B	CST/B	OUTS	@	COST	RETAIL	% COST
1.	GORDONS	.83	26.67	3.880	32.00	.40	.121	.346	34.97
2.	CHERRY BRANDY	.83	24.60	3.200	28.81	.60	.108	.507	21.30
3.	SODA	7.00	40.00	.180	1.00	.50	.031	.076	40.79
4.	LEMON JUICE	1.00	72.00	1.320			.018		
5.	LEMON SLICE	1.00	8.00	.080			.010		
6.									
7.									
8.									
9.									
10.	STRAW,COCKTAILSTICK						.015		
11.									
		TOTAL COST					.303	.929	32.62
12.		SALE PRICE		1.30	(inc VAT)		26.80%		

....

		LAST COST						% INC	

A computerised version of the cocktail costed manually on page 62.

DATE: 28.11.81 BAR:ONE

COCKTAIL NAME: SINGAPORE GIN SLING

	INGREDIENTS	OZS	OZ/B	CST/B	OUTS	@	COST	RETAIL	% COST
1.	GORDONS	.83	26.67	5.600	32.00	.70	.174	.606	28.71
2.	CHERRY BRANDY	.83	24.60	5.570	28.81	1.25	.188	1.057	17.79
3.	SODA	7.00	40.00	.250	1.00	1.00	.044	.152	28.95
4.	LEMON JUICE	1.00	72.00	1.760			.024		
5.	LEMON SLICE	1.00	8.00	.100			.012		
6.									
7.									
8.									
9.									
10.	STRAW,COCKTAILSTICK						.018		
11.									
		TOTAL COST					.460	1.815	25.34
12.		SALE PRICE		2.30	(inc VAT)		23.00%		

....

		LAST COST 24.10.79					.303	% INC	51.81

The same cocktail recosted after two years with a cost percentage increase record.

15 Examples of calculations

Although nearly everybody understands what percentages are, I would like to clarify what one means by the term. So many *per cent* (%) means so many one hundredth parts. One per cent is one hundredth part of any figure. For example:

$$7 \text{ per cent of } £100 = \frac{7 \times 1 \times £100}{100} = £7$$

If one understands this principle, it is easy to follow the following exercises which arise during the week's work of any manager or controller in every food and beverage outlet.

1 The potential revenue of Bar One was £3622.12 (representing 100%). The potential revenue increase due to measure increases was 27.3%. What was the new potential revenue?

$$100\% = £3622.12$$
$$127.3\% = ?$$
$$\frac{3622.12 \times 127.3}{100} = £4610.96$$

2 Due to tax deduction the selling price of a bottle of wine was reduced by 23%. The bottle is now £6.80 a bottle. How much was the original price?

$$\frac{6.80 \times 100}{77} = £8.83$$

3 How much is 5/12 in decimals?

$$\frac{5}{12} = 0.4166$$

4 How much is the weight of one gallon of Guinness? When the empty weight is 38 lbs, the full weight is 131 lbs, and the container is 9 gallons?

131 lbs	Full weight
− 38 lbs	Empty weight
93 lbs	Contents

$$\frac{93 \text{ lbs}}{9 \text{ gallon}} = 10.33 \text{ lbs or } 10 \text{ lbs } 5 \text{ oz}$$

$$0.33 \times 16 = 5.28 \text{ oz } (5 \text{ oz})$$

5 As you see on page 44, the potential sales of Scotch Whiskies was £518.20 for Bar One. This represents 14.31 (rounded up) of the total potential sales which were namely £3622.12. Due to the measure increase the selling price was increased equally by 50%. What was:

a) The % uplift?
b) The increase of the total potential new revenue in money terms?
c) The new potential revenue of Scotch Whisky?

a) $\dfrac{14.31 \times 150}{100} = 21.46\%$

b) $\dfrac{3622.12 \times 7.15}{100} = £258.98$

c) $\dfrac{518.20 \times 21.46}{14.31} = £777.12$

or:

£518.20 + £258.98 = £777.18

The difference of 0.06 is due to rounding up.

6 One Litre of wine cost £1.32. How much would 75 cl cost? One litre = 100 cl. Therefore the formula should be:

$$\frac{£1.32 \times 75 \text{ cl}}{100} = £0.99$$

7 A Barrel of Beer cost £56.16. How much would be the cost of 1 pint?

One Barrel = 36 gallons = 288 pints

$$\frac{£56.16}{288 \text{ pints}} = 19.5\text{p}$$

8 A French table wine cost 1800 francs per barrique. How much is the cost of 1 litre before bottling if the currency exchange rate is 9.07 francs for £1 Sterling?

A Barrique = 225 litres.

$$\frac{100 \text{ pence} \times 1800 \text{ francs}}{9.07 \text{ francs} \times 100 \times 225} = 88.2\text{p}$$

9 A Doppel Ohm of Moselle wine costs, before bottling, 1224 DM. How much would a 70 cl bottle be if the currency exchange rate is 3.92 DM for £1 Sterling?

A Doppel Ohm = 300 litres

$$\frac{100 \text{ pence} \times 1224 \text{ DM} \times 70}{3.92 \text{ DM} \times 100 \times 300 \times 100} = 72.9\text{p}$$

10 If one wishes to give two per cent of the total beverage revenue (see page 43) as an incentive for the bar staff, how much would each individual member get with the following points system?

2 Head Bar Men	3 points each			6
2 Assistant Head Bar Men	2½	"	"	5
14 Bar Men	2	"	"	28
2 Porters	1½	"	"	3
20				42

						Pay each
2 Head Bar Men	3 points each			6	124.68	62.34
2 Ass. Head Bar Men	2½	"	"	5	103.90	51.95
14 Bar Men	2	"	"	28	581.34	41.56
2 Porters	1½	"	"	3	62.34	31.17
20 TOTAL	=			42	£872.76	20.78

So one point is equivalent to £20.78:

$$\frac{43645 \times 2}{100} = 872.90 \qquad \frac{872.9}{42} = 20.78$$

11 What are the following cost percentages?

	Cost	Revenue
a) Bar One	1150.77	3722.98
b) Bar Two	735.29	2600.78
c) Bar Three	303.21	852.07
d) Bar Four	628.54	2104.00
e) Bar Five	170.77	520.42
f) Total	£2989.21	£9800.25

$$\frac{\text{Cost} \times 100}{\text{Revenue}} = \text{Cost }\%$$

a) 30.91%
b) 28.3%
c) 35.59%
d) 29.87%
e) 32.81%
f) 30.5%

12 The total beverage revenue includes eight per cent VAT and ten per cent Service Charge. How much was the nett revenue if total revenue was £11642.70?

$$\frac{11642.70 \times 100 \times 100}{108 \times 100} = £9800.25$$

13 Establish the exact liquid amount left in a keg of Murphy's if the weight of the container with Beer was 100 lbs. The empty container weight is 19 lbs and the weight of one gallon is 10.2 lbs (10 lbs 3 oz).

	100 lbs	container and beer weight
Less	19 lbs	container weight
	81 lbs	weight of beer

$$\frac{81}{10.2} = 7.94 \text{ (rounded up to 8) gallons}$$

14 The cost of a bottle of wine is £1.58. How much would be the selling price if the cost percentage is 35%?

$$\frac{1.58 \times 100}{35} = £4.51\tfrac{1}{2}$$

15 The selling price of a bottle of wine inclusive of 8% VAT is £7.85. The cost is £2.36. What would be the cost percentage?

$$\frac{7.85 \times 100}{108} = 7.2681$$

$$\frac{2.36 \times 100}{7.2681} = 32.47\%$$

16 What is 40° Celsius expressed in Fahrenheit?

$$\frac{40°C \times 9}{5} = 72 + 32 = 104°F$$

17 What is 50° Fahrenheit expressed in Celsius?

$$50 - 32 = 18$$

$$\frac{18 \times 5}{9} = 10°C$$

18 The four-weekly beverage report shows a total actual turnover of £43 645 for all bars. The cost was £13 639, which includes a fruit cost of £171.

a) How much was the actual turnover inclusive of 8% VAT?
b) How much was the cost percentage inclusive of fruit cost?
c) How much was the cost percentage exclusive of fruit cost?

a) $$\frac{43645 \times 108}{100} = £47136.60$$

b) $$\frac{13639 \times 100}{43645} = 31.25\%$$

c) $$\frac{13468 \times 100}{43645} = 30.86\%$$

19 Bar One had a total fruit cost of £28.68. How much does this represent as a percentage of the total cost of £1150.77?

$$\frac{£28.68 \times 100}{£1150.77} = 2.49\%$$

20 Express the increase due to changes of measures from $^1/_6$ of a gill to $^1/_4$ of a gill as a percentage (1 gill = 5 fluid ounces).

$$\frac{5 \text{ ozs}}{4} = 1.25 \text{ Fluid ozs}$$

$$\frac{5 \text{ ozs}}{6} = 0.833 \text{ Fluid ozs}$$

$$1.25 - 0.833 = 0.417$$

$$\frac{0.417 \times 100}{0.833} = 50.06\% \text{ Increase}$$

21 The total bread cost on Thursday, 11th November, 1979 was £115.68. A thirty per cent discount was already allowed. How much was the discount?

$$\frac{£115.68 \times 30\%}{70} = £49.58$$

22 Fifteen per cent VAT is included in the total food revenue of £48 648.35. How much is the revenue excluding VAT?

$$\frac{£48648.35 \times 100}{115} = £42302.91$$

23 The selling price of a menu is £6.50 inclusive of VAT at fifteen per cent. How much is the cost of the menu when the gross profit is sixty-two per cent?

$$\frac{6.50 \times 100}{115} = \frac{5.65 \times 62}{100} = 3.50$$

$$5.65 - 3.50 = £2.15$$

Selling price	£6.50 (incl. of VAT)	
	£5.65 (excl. of VAT)	
Gross profit	£3.50	62%
Cost	£2.15	38%

24 At the top of page 148 are courses of a meal expressed as proportion of the total cost of the meal.

The main dish cost is £1.30. How much is the total cost of the menu and the cost of the unproductive items?

$$\frac{1.30 \times 100}{55} = £2.36$$

$$\frac{2.36 \times 5}{100} = 11.8p = 12p \text{ (rounded up)}$$

Items	*Proportion of total cost*
	%
Hors d'oeuvre	10
Main Dish	55
Vegetables	8
Potatoes	4
Sweet	8
Beverages	6
Bread and Butter	4
Unproductive items	5
Total	100

25 If you mix four different coffee beans at the prices of £1.49, £1.64, £1.52 and £1.59 per pound in equal parts how much is the cost of one pound?

$$\frac{1.49 + 1.64 + 1.52 + 1.59}{4} = £1.56$$

16 Useful information

Bottle sizes (Champagne capacity)

Quart	20 cl	
Half	40 cl	
Bottle	80 cl	
Magnum	2 Bottles	
Jeroboam	4 Bottles	
Rehoboam	6 Bottles	
Mathusalum ×	8 Bottles	METHUSELAH
Salmanazar	12 Bottles	
Balthazar	16 Bottles	
Nabuchodonosor ×	20 Bottles	NEBUCHADNEZZAR.

Bottle sizes

Germany		70 cl
France	Alsace	72 cl
	Anjou	75 cl
	Bordeaux	75 cl
	Burgundy	75 cl
	Brandy	70 cl
Portugal	Port	70 cl
Spain	Sherry	70 cl
Madeira	Madeira	70 cl
England	Whisky	75 cl

Capacity and volume

Pints		**Litres**
1.761	1	0.568
3.521	2	1.136
5.282	3	1.704
7.043	4	2.272
8.804	5	2.840
10.564	6	3.408
12.325	7	3.976
14.086	8	4.544
15.847	9	5.112

1 To convert gallons to litres, multiply by 4.546
2 To convert litres to gallons, multiply by .22

1 pint = 20 fluid ounces = 0.568 litres
1 fluid ounce = 28.4 cm^3 = 0.0284 litres
5 fluid ounces = 1 gill = 0.142 litres
1 quart = 2 pints = 1.136 litres

Cask sizes (capacity)

				Used in
Germany	stück	=	1200 litres	Franken
	halbstück	=	600 litres	Rheingau
	viertelstück	=	300 litres	Hessen
	fuder	=	1000 litres	Pfalz
	fuder	=	960 litres	Moselle
	fuder	=	900 litres	Franken
	fuder	=	1500 litres	Baden
	ohm	=	150 litres	In nearly all districts
	doppel ohm	=	300 litres	In nearly all districts
	ohm	=	160 litres	Moselle
	logel	=	40 litres	Pfalz
	eimer	=	300 litres	Württemberg
France	aume	=	114 litres	Alsace
	piece	=	220 litres	Anjou
	piece	=	228 litres	Burgundy
	barrique	=	225 litres	Bordeaux
Spain	butt	=	490.7 litres	Sherry
Portugal	pipe	=	522.5 litres	Port
Madeira	pipe	=	418 litres	Madeira

Weights

1 ounce	=	16 drams
1 pound	=	16 ounces
1 stone	=	14 pounds
1 quarter	=	28 pounds
1 hundredweight	=	4 quarters
1 ton	=	20 hundredweights

pounds		**kilograms**
2.2046	1	0.45359
4.4092	2	0.90718
6.6139	3	1.36078
8.8185	4	1.81437
11.0231	5	2.26796
13.2277	6	2.72155
15.4324	7	3.17515
17.6370	8	3.62874
19.8416	9	4.08233

1 To convert pounds to kilograms, multiply by 0.45359
2 To convert kilograms to pounds, multiply by 2.2046

1 pound = 16 ounces = 0.45359 KG
1 ounce = 28.350 grams

Can sizes

type of can	**approximate net weight**
baby can	4½ oz
5 oz	5 oz
8 oz	8 oz
A1	10 oz
A1	14 oz
No 1 tall	1 lb
1 lb flat	1 lb
A 2	1¼ lb
A 2½	1¾ lb
3 lb H.R.	3 lb
A 1O	6¾ lb

Temperatures

Frozen meats	−18°C to −20°C
Frozen vegetables	−10°C to −15°C
Ice creams	− 2°C to − 3°C
Refrigerators	3°C to 4°C
Blast coolers	4°C
Cooling areas	6°C to 8°C
Kitchen environment	18°C to 24°C
Hot cabinets and bain marie	75°C to 85°C